DK | SMITHSONIAN

Did You Know?
Ocean

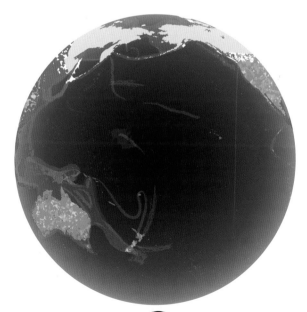

SMITHSONIAN
INSTITUTION

Established in 1846, the Smithsonian Institution—the world's largest museum and research complex—includes 19 museums and galleries and the National Zoological Park. The total number of artifacts, works of art, and specimens in the Smithsonian's collection is estimated at 155 million, the bulk of which is contained in the National Museum of Natural History, which holds more than 126 million specimens and objects. The Smithsonian is a renowned research center, dedicated to public education, national service, and scholarship in the arts, sciences, and history.

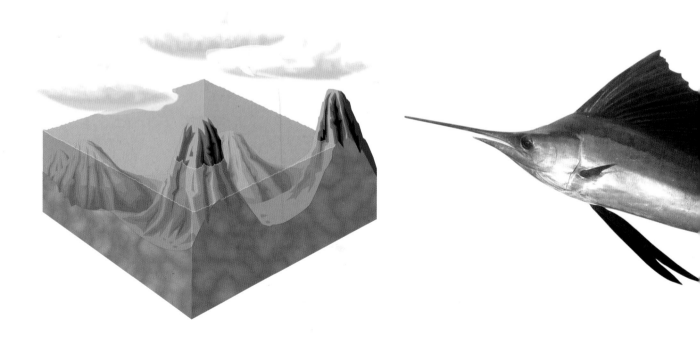

DK SMITHSONIAN

Did You Know?
Ocean

Steve Setford

Author Steve Setford
Consultant Derek Harvey
Smithsonian Consultant Dr. Dave Pawson
Senior Scientist, Emeritus, Curator of Echinoderms
National Museum of Natural History, Smithsonian
Illustrator Dan Crisp

DK LONDON
Senior Editor Marie Greenwood
Senior Art Editor Ann Cannings
US Editor Margaret Parrish
US Senior Editor Shannon Beatty
Managing Editor Jonathan Melmoth
Managing Art Editor Diane Peyton Jones
Production Editor Dragana Puvacic
Production Controller Magdalena Bojko
Jacket Designer Ann Cannings
Publishing Coordinator Issy Walsh
Deputy Art Director Mabel Chan
Publishing Director Sarah Larter

DK DELHI
Senior Editor Roohi Sehgal
Senior Art Editor Nidhi Mehra
Project Art Editor Kanika Kalra
Art Editor Bhagyashree Nayak
Managing Editor Monica Saigal
Managing Art Editor Romi Chakraborty
Jacket Designer Dheeraj Arora
DTP Designers Dheeraj Singh, Syed Md Farhan
CTS Manager Balwant Singh
Production Manager Pankaj Sharma
Project Picture Researcher Sakshi Saluja
Delhi Creative Heads Glenda Fernandes,
Malavika Talukder

First American edition, 2022
Published in the United States by DK Publishing
1450 Broadway, Suite 801, New York, NY 10018

MIX
Paper from
responsible sources
FSC™ C018179

This book was made with Forest
Stewardship Council™ certified paper—
one small step in DK's commitment to
a sustainable future. For more information
go to www.dk.com/our-green-pledge

SMITHSONIAN

Contents

The blue planet

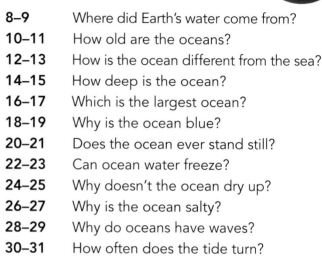

Ocean features

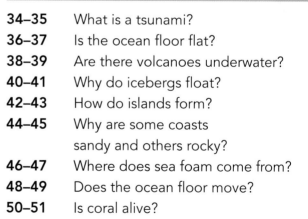

Ocean habitats

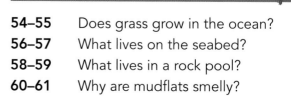

Find out how birds survive at sea on page 100.

Oceans and us

Ocean life

Find out why polar animals don't freeze on page 70.

? Quick quiz

Test your knowledge! Look for the "Quick quiz" boxes throughout this book to see how much you've learned. You'll find some of the answers on the pages, but you may have to look up or make your best guess for the others. Turn to pages 132–133 for the answers.

The blue planet

Seen from space, Earth is a blue planet—a world covered mostly by salty water. Since the first oceans formed, they have been constantly on the move, whipped by winds into waves and pulled by the moon into tides, with currents surging at the surface and deep below.

Where did Earth's water come from?

About 4.5 billion years ago, when Earth first formed, water was probably already present in the rocks that clumped together to create the planet. This water was released and found its way to the surface. The rest of Earth's water came from space.

Clouds form

Gases and water vapor formed Earth's early atmosphere. As the atmosphere cooled, the water vapor condensed into clouds.

Water vapor hung in Earth's atmosphere until Earth cooled below 212°F (100°C) and then the first rain came.

Volcanic eruptions

Young Earth was covered with volcanoes. When the volcanoes erupted, they spewed out hot gases and water vapor from deep below the surface.

Water from space

Some water was brought to the young Earth by rocky meteorites and balls of dust, gas, and ice called comets that struck the planet.

Comet

How does ocean water stay on Earth?

Earth's gravity is a force that pulls everything toward the ground. Gravity stops the oceans from flying off into space, just as it keeps water in a glass when you pour it.

? Quick quiz

1. What was Earth's early atmosphere made of?

2. Why don't the oceans fly off into space?

See pages 132–133 for the answers

Rain falls

Rain fell and vast hollows on Earth's surface filled with water. The land was now cool enough for the water to stay as liquid and not evaporate.

Oceans form

The water-filled hollows became the first oceans. The rain dissolved salt from the rocks, which made the ocean water salty.

Water world (4.4 bya)

About 150 million years after Earth formed, a single ocean covered the whole planet. A billion years later, tiny organisms called microbes appeared in the sea—the first life on Earth.

How old are the oceans?

There have been oceans for most of Earth's 4.5-billion-year history. During that time, old oceans disappeared and new ones formed. As the planet warmed up, sea levels rose.

KEY
bya = billion years ago; mya = million years ago

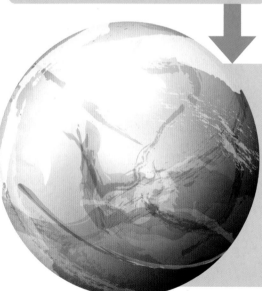

Snowball Earth (700 mya)

Millions of years later, the vast ocean froze over and a deep-freeze gripped Earth. Sea levels plummeted. This ice age lasted for more than 100 million years.

What used to live in the oceans?

Helicoprion

The sharklike Helicoprion lived 270 mya. It had a whorl of teeth as big as a dinner plate in its lower jaw. The toothy whorl looked like a saw-toothed pizza cutter!

Ichthyosaurus

This sleek reptile predator cruised the ocean 190 mya. Its streamlined, muscly body helped it to swim quickly in search of prey, such as fish, squid, and other marine reptiles.

? True or false?

1. Ichthyosaurus was a type of fish.

2. The single vast ocean of 230 mya was called Pangaea.

3. Sea levels fell during the great ice age 700 mya.

See pages 132–133 for the answers

Oceans today

Because the continents never stop moving, the oceans are still changing. The Atlantic Ocean is growing, while the Pacific Ocean is shrinking—but only by an inch or so each year.

Panthalassic Ocean (230 mya)

All Earth's landmasses were joined as a single super continent called Pangaea. It was surrounded by one vast ocean, the Panthalassic Ocean. Pangaea eventually broke up.

Ice melts (100 mya)

Earth grew so warm that glaciers and ice at the poles melted. Liquid water entered the ocean and sea levels rose. Much of the land became covered by ocean.

Oceans change (66 mya)

The oceans changed in size and shape as the continents drifted slowly over the Earth's surface. Earth began to look more and more like the planet we know today.

How is the ocean different from the sea?

Both oceans and seas are large areas of salt water, although oceans are much bigger than seas. The salt water that covers nearly two-thirds of Earth's surface is divided into five oceans and more than 50 seas.

Ocean

Oceans are so vast and deep that large areas remain unexplored. The oceans separate Earth's continents.

Sea

A sea is smaller and shallower than an ocean. Most seas lie at the edges of oceans and are partly landlocked or surrounded by land.

Partly landlocked

Irish Sea

Shallower

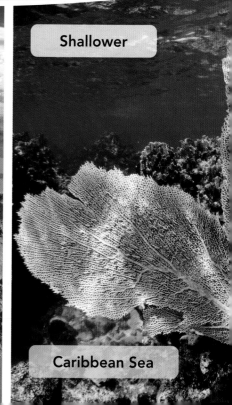

Caribbean Sea

Where are the world's oceans?

There are five named oceans, and they are all connected. The Arctic Ocean covers the North Pole, while the Southern Ocean encircles the South Pole. Between them, roughly around Earth's middle, lie the Pacific, Atlantic, and Indian oceans.

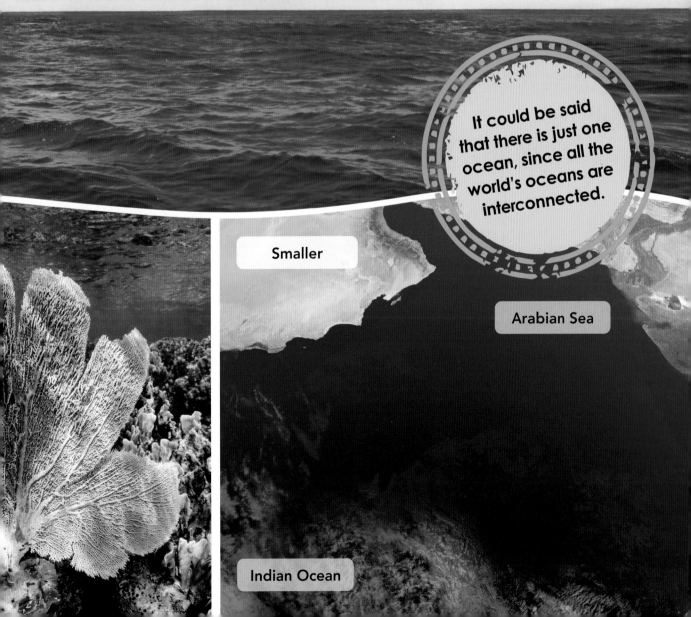

It could be said that there is just one ocean, since all the world's oceans are interconnected.

Smaller

Arabian Sea

Indian Ocean

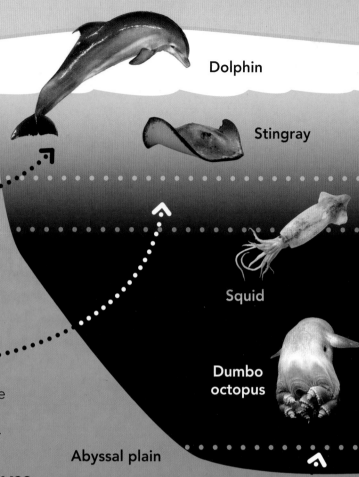

Continental shelf

Dolphin

Stingray

Sunlit zone
0–650 ft (0–200 m)
Bathed in sunlight, the surface layer is rich in life. Winds, tides, and currents keep it moving. The water's temperature may change with the seasons.

Squid

Twilight zone
650–3,300 ft (200–1,000 m)
It is gloomy here, but there is just enough light to see. At night, some animals swim up to the surface to feed, then swim back down by day.

Dumbo octopus

Abyssal plain

Abyss
13,000–20,000 ft (4,000–6,000 m)
Here, there is only eerie, near-freezing, inky blackness. The weight of the water above presses with immense force on the animals of the abyss.

How deep is the ocean?

The depth of the ocean varies greatly, from shallow coastal waters to underwater canyons around 7 miles (11 km) below the surface. The deeper you go, the darker and colder it gets, and the more the water above presses upon you.

? Picture quiz

What zone does this stingray live in?

See pages 132–133 for the answer

What is an ocean's deepest point ?

The deepest place we know of is in the Mariana Trench, in the Western Pacific Ocean. At a place called the Challenger Deep, the ocean floor is 36,200 ft (11,030 m) below the surface.

Seahorse

650 ft (200 m)

3,300 ft (1,000 m)

Midnight zone
3,300–13,000 ft (1,000–4,000 m)
The midnight zone is cold and utterly dark.
Many animals can make their own light to help
them find food or mates, or to scare off predators.

Tripod fish

Frilled shark

13,000 ft (4,000 m)

Hadal zone
Below 20,000 ft (6,000 m)
At plunging chasms called
ocean trenches, the seafloor
drops down to mind-boggling
depths. Amazingly, a few animals
still manage to survive here.

20,000 ft
(6,000 m)

Trench

The Mariana Trench
is 2 miles (3 km)
deeper than Mount
Everest is tall!

29,500 ft (9,000 m)

33,000 ft (10,000 m)

36,000 ft (11,000 m)

Which is the largest ocean?

The Pacific is the largest and deepest of Earth's five oceans. Scattered islands dot its open waters, which are rich in marine life. Around the edges of the Pacific lie deep trenches and many active volcanoes.

Deep trenches

In the Western Pacific, the ocean floor is being pushed down into Earth's interior and destroyed, creating a line of deep trenches.

Pacific Ocean

Coral islands

Thousands of coral islands pepper the warm South Pacific. These islands are formed around the peaks of volcanoes that erupted from the seabed.

Great Barrier Reef

The world's largest coral reef is so big it can be seen from space. It runs for 1,430 miles (2,300 km) along Australia's northeast coast.

Sea life

The cool Northeast Pacific waters are rich in plankton. Seabirds and whales feast on the vast schools of fish that arrive to feed on the plankton.

? Quick quiz

1. Which is larger, the Southern or the Indian ocean?

2. What is the name of the world's largest coral reef?

3. What feeds on plankton in the Northeast Pacific?

See pages 132–133 for the answers

Hawaiian Islands

In the middle of the Pacific lie the Hawaiian Islands. They were formed from huge underwater volcanoes, some of which are still active today.

How large is the Pacific Ocean?

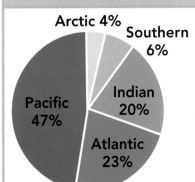

Arctic 4%
Southern 6%
Pacific 47%
Indian 20%
Atlantic 23%

The Pacific is roughly equal to the combined size of the other four oceans. It is more than twice the size of the Atlantic, the next largest ocean, and nearly 12 times bigger than the Arctic, the smallest of the five oceans.

Why is the ocean blue?

Sunlight contains many different colors. When the light shines down on the sea, each color enters the water and reaches a different depth before being absorbed. The blue light travels deepest and then scatters—making the water appear blue.

Shallowest color.

Red light is absorbed within the first 33 ft (10 m). By 165 ft (50 m), orange and yellow have disappeared, too.

Why is the ocean sometimes green?

Tiny plantlike algae in the water can make it look green. Algae use a chemical called chlorophyll to capture energy from sunlight. Chlorophyll reflects green light, giving the water a greenish tint.

Deepest color

Blue light reaches about 3,300 ft (1,000 m). As it travels, it gets scattered in every direction.

Sunlight

Although sunshine looks white, it contains all the colors of the spectrum. We see these colors when falling rain splits sunlight into a rainbow.

When is water colorless?

Water looks colorless in small amounts, such as a glassful. Light passes through the water without being affected. The deeper the water, the more colors it absorbs and the bluer it looks.

Absorbing colors

The different colors get absorbed into the ocean water. Some colors are absorbed near the surface, others deeper down.

330 ft (100 m)

Deeper still

Beyond the reach of the blue light, the ocean is as dark as night.

3,300 ft (1,000 m)

? *True or false?*

1. Green light travels deepest in the ocean.

2. Sunlight is made up of many different colors.

3. Tiny plantlike algae turn seawater purple.

See pages 132–133 for the answers

Warm currents

On the western sides of the oceans, surface currents carry warm water from the tropical areas around Earth's middle toward colder regions.

The California Current carries cold water down the eastern side of the Pacific Ocean.

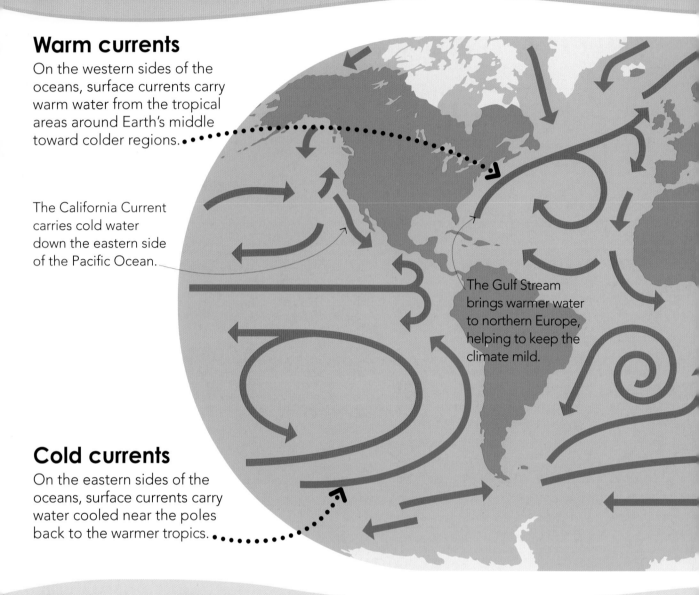

The Gulf Stream brings warmer water to northern Europe, helping to keep the climate mild.

Cold currents

On the eastern sides of the oceans, surface currents carry water cooled near the poles back to the warmer tropics.

Does the ocean ever stand still?

No. Driven by the wind, changes in water temperature, and Earth's rotation, ocean water is constantly flowing around the globe in giant streams called currents. Some currents flow at the surface, others along the seafloor.

What can bath ducks teach us about currents?

In 1992, a cargo of 29,000 bath toys, including yellow ducks, was lost at sea. They washed up in different places around the world. Their journeys have helped scientists to map ocean currents.

In some places, currents link up to form circular flows called gyres.

The Antarctic Circumpolar is a cold current that flows around Antarctica.

? True or false?

1. Currents are partly driven by Earth's rotation.

2. The Gulf Stream brings cold water to northern Europe.

3. Gyres are circular currents that link up.

See pages 132–133 for the answers

The Kuroshio Current carries warm water up the side of the North Pacific.

Deep water can take 1,000 years to travel from the North Atlantic to the North Pacific!

Some of the ducks may still be at sea!

What is the Global Conveyer Belt?

As warm tropical water (red) chills when it reaches the North Atlantic, it gets denser and heavier and so sinks. It then flows as a deep cold current (blue) along the ocean floor, before rising back up. This system is called the Global Conveyer Belt.

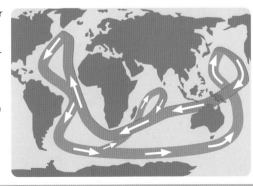

Can ocean water freeze?

It can—especially around the North and South poles, where bitter winds chill the ocean's surface. Ponds and lakes freeze at 32°F (0°C), but the salt in seawater stops the sea from freezing until the temperature falls to 28.4°F (-2°C).

Icebreaker

Icebreakers are ships with toughened hulls and powerful engines. These allow them to force their way through great slabs of ice called pack ice.

Breathing hole

Weddell seals hunt under the ice. They use claws on their front flippers to make holes in the ice so that they can come up for air.

Under the ice

Algae growing on the underside of the ice provide food for shrimplike krill. Fish, such as this bald rockcod, eat the krill.

How much sea ice is there?

The amount of sea ice in the ocean varies. It is at its peak at the end of winter, as a lot melts in summer. Because of global warming, Earth is heating up and the area of the ocean that freezes is getting smaller.

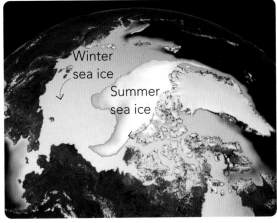

Winter sea ice

Summer sea ice

Ice in the Arctic

? Quick quiz

1. What are round plates of sea ice called?
   a) waffle ice
   b) pancake ice
   c) pack ice

2. How cold does the ocean have to be to freeze?
   a) 32°F (0°C)
   b) 212°F (100°C)
   c) 28.4°F (-2°C)

See pages 132–133 for the answers

What happens when the ocean freezes?

At the poles each winter, the open sea slowly changes into a layer of solid ice. In the south, around Antarctica, ice forms near the shore. At the North Pole, ice that has survived the summer spreads over the Arctic Ocean again.

5. Sea ice that freezes to the shore is called fast ice. Floating ice that is not fast to the land is called pack ice.

1. Tiny ice crystals start to grow near the surface, giving the water a greasy, slushy look.

4. Ice floes freeze together again as thick, jumbled masses of drifting pack ice.

2. Waves clump ice crystals together into round plates called pancake ice.

3. The ice joins up to form sheets. Waves break the sheets into slabs called floes.

Why doesn't the ocean dry up?

The sun's energy drives the water cycle.

Lots of water leaves the ocean when it gets warmed by the sun, but it is always replaced by water from rain, snow, and the land. Water is continually circulating between the ocean, air, and land in a never-ending process called the water cycle.

Evaporation

The sun warms water at the ocean's surface. The water evaporates—it turns from a liquid into a gas. The gas is called water vapor.

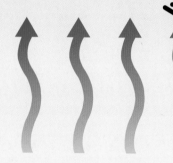

Water evaporates from the surface of the sea.

Will there always be an ocean?

No! Near the end of its life, the sun will grow brighter and swell to many times its present size. Earth will get so hot that all its water will evaporate, leaving the planet dry. Luckily, that won't happen for at least a billion years!

Clouds

Water vapor in the air rises and cools. It condenses, turning back into tiny droplets of liquid water. The floating droplets form clouds.

Rain

The water droplets in the clouds join up to make bigger drops. They eventually fall as rain. If they freeze, they form snowflakes.

? True or false?

1. When water evaporates, it turns from gas into liquid.

2. Earth will always have an ocean.

3. The water cycle is the movement of water between the ocean, atmosphere, and land.

See pages 132–133 for the answers

Land flow

Rain and melted snow run over land and into rivers, streams, and lakes. Rivers eventually empty their water into the ocean.

Trees draw water from the soil and release it into the air from their leaves.

Groundwater

Some water seeps below the surface and makes its way through underground rocks until it flows into the ocean.

The amount of water on Earth doesn't change—it just gets used again and again.

Why is the ocean salty?

The salt in seawater is the same as the salt we use in our food. It is the mineral sodium chloride. Salt gets washed from the land into the sea and dissolves easily. The first seas were probably only slightly salty. As rain washed more salt into the sea over billions of years, the oceans grew saltier.

Freed from rock

Falling rain dissolves salt and other minerals from rocks and soil. The water runs over land, taking the salt with it. It eventually flows into rivers.

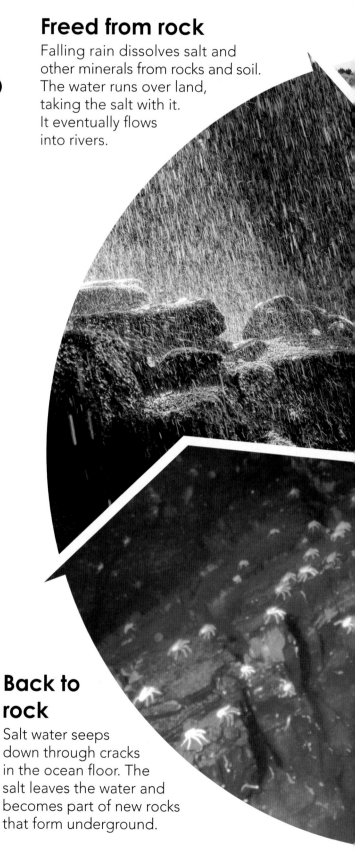

How much salt is there in the ocean?

If all the salt could be extracted from the ocean and put on land, it would cover the surface in a layer of salt about 500 ft (150 m) thick—as high as a 40-story building!

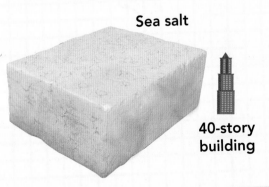

Sea salt

40-story building

Back to rock

Salt water seeps down through cracks in the ocean floor. The salt leaves the water and becomes part of new rocks that form underground.

Carried by rivers

Rivers carry the dissolved salt toward the sea. There is only a tiny amount of salt in river water, which is why it doesn't taste salty like seawater.

Into the sea

Rivers empty water into the sea, adding salt to the ocean. Marine organisms take salt into their bodies, and some salt settles and becomes part of the ocean floor.

About 97 percent of Earth's water is salty and most of it is in the ocean.

Can we drink seawater?

It's not safe to drink seawater because our bodies can't cope with the high levels of salt it contains. However, we can remove the salt to get drinkable fresh water. This is done at desalination plants on the coast.

Why do oceans have waves?

Waves form when wind pushes against the ocean's surface, making the water rise and fall. First, ripples form out in the ocean. These grow into waves as the wind continues to blow. Waves travel over the ocean before breaking. Tides also cause the water to rise and fall along the shore.

Bobbing bird

It might look as if waves move water forward, but they don't. Just watch a seabird bobbing up and down on the waves—like the water beneath, it does not move forward.

Wind

The wind passes some of its energy to the water. The harder the wind blows, the more energy the water gains.

The highest wave ever surfed was more than 80 ft (24 m) tall!

Water motion

The water in each wave goes around in circles. It passes energy to the water in front, moving the wave forward.

How do waves break on the shore?

A wave crashing, or breaking, onto the shore is called a breaker. As a wave nears the shore, its base hits the seabed and slows down. But the crest continues at the same speed, so the wave starts to lean forward. Eventually, the wave topples and breaks.

? Picture quiz

What are waves called when they collapse onto the shore?

See pages 132–133 for the answers

Crest

The top of a wave is called the crest. The distance between two crests is the length of the wave.

Still water level

This is the level of the ocean's surface when no wind is blowing and the water is calm.

Trough

The dip between two crests is called a trough. The height of the wave is the distance from trough to crest.

Earth

Our planet makes
one complete turn
every day, sweeping
each ocean through
two high tides
and two low tides.

Low tide

High tide

Earth rotating

How often
does the tide turn?

Low tide

The tide generally turns every six hours. Each
day there are two high tides, when the ocean
rises, and two low tides, when it falls back
again. Tides are caused by the moon's gravity,
and by the way the Earth spins around.

Low tide

On either side
of Earth between
the bulges, the
gravitational pull
is weaker and the
sea level falls. This
is where we get
low tides.

Moon's gravity

Gravity is an invisible force of attraction between objects. The moon's gravity pulls on Earth, and Earth's gravity pulls on the moon, too.

High tide

High tide

Where Earth faces the moon, gravity tugs the sea into a bulge called a high tide. On Earth's opposite side, the sea is flung out into a second bulge.

What happens at high and low tides?

At high tide, the sea comes in and water covers the land. At low tide, the sea retreats, uncovering sand, mud, and rocks. Many shore creatures bury themselves, hide in rock pools, or move out to deeper water.

High tide

Low tide

Can tides be dangerous?

Tides can rise so quickly that people can get stranded, so it is always important to check when high tides are due. When tidal water rushes through channels, it can create whirlpools. These powerful swirls of water can pull swimmers into their center and suck them under.

Whirlpool at Saltstraumen in Norway

? Quick quiz

1. How many hours does it take for the tide to turn?

2. What force pulls the ocean into a high tide?

3. How many low tides are there each day?

See pages 132–133 for the answers

Ocean features

Every day, the ocean is sculpting our coastlines. New islands are thrust above the waves and coral reefs form along the shore. The ocean floor is always changing, too. Undersea volcanoes erupt, cracks appear on the seabed, and mountains grow in the depths.

What is a tsunami?

Tsunamis are immensely powerful waves that race across the ocean at up to 500 mph (800 kph). Unlike normal waves, tsunamis are not formed by winds. They are usually triggered by earthquakes at sea, and sometimes by underwater landslides and volcanic eruptions.

Dangerous waves

Tsunami waves can be over 100 ft (30 m) high. When they strike the coast, they can demolish houses, uproot trees, carry off vehicles, and cause flooding.

What does "tsunami" mean?

Tsunami means "harbor wave" in Japanese. Japan is especially prone to tsunamis because it lies in part of the Pacific Ocean called the "Ring of Fire," where many earthquakes and volcanic eruptions occur.

How does a tsunami form?

When an earthquake shakes the ocean floor, the water above is pushed upward. This sets off surface waves that spread out like ripples. The high-energy waves grow bigger the closer they get to the shore.

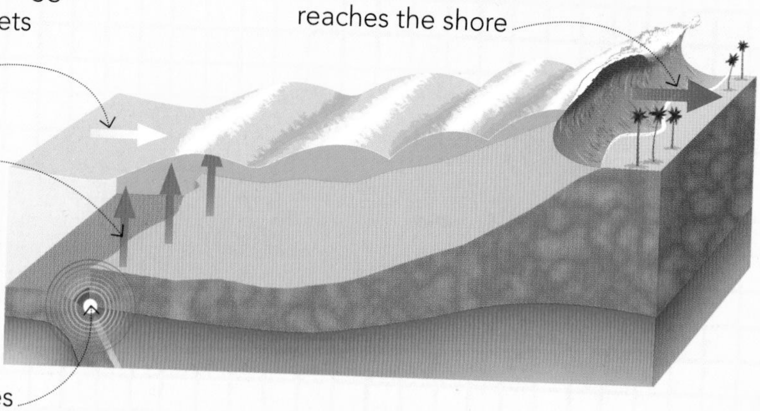

Waves get bigger as water gets shallower.

Huge wall of water reaches the shore

Water is pushed up.

Shockwaves spread out.

? True or false?

1. Tsunamis are formed by strong winds at sea.

2. "Tsunami" means "island wave."

3. Tsunami waves get bigger as the water gets deeper.

See pages 132–133 for the answers

Is the ocean floor flat?

Yes… and no! Nearly three-quarters of the ocean floor is made up of vast plains that include some of the flattest areas on Earth. However, in other places there are steep slopes and deep trenches, mountain ranges and lone peaks, and both active and extinct volcanoes.

There are maps of Mars that are more detailed than those of the ocean floor!

Ocean trench

Where two tectonic plates collide, a long, narrow, V-shaped trench forms. A trench has very steep sides and is incredibly deep.

Mid-ocean ridge

A ridge of underwater mountains forms where two tectonic plates pull apart. The mountains lie on either side of a long crack in the seabed.

Continental shelf

What are tectonic plates?

These are the great rocky slabs that make up Earth's crust. They fit together like puzzle pieces. The magma beneath them is always moving. This churning moves the plates over Earth's surface.

Continental crust

Oceanic crust

What is the tallest ocean mountain?

Mauna Kea, in Hawaii. This monster mountain pokes up above the waves, but more than half of it is underwater. Measured from the seafloor to its summit, Mauna Kea is taller than Everest, the highest mountain on land.

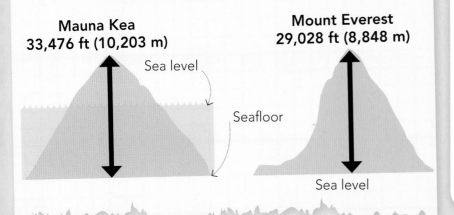

Mauna Kea
33,476 ft (10,203 m)

Sea level

Seafloor

Mount Everest
29,028 ft (8,848 m)

Sea level

? Picture quiz

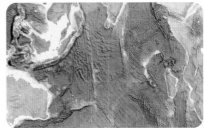

What is this long ocean floor feature called?

a) seamount

b) mid-ocean ridge

c) volcanic island

See pages 132–133 for the answer

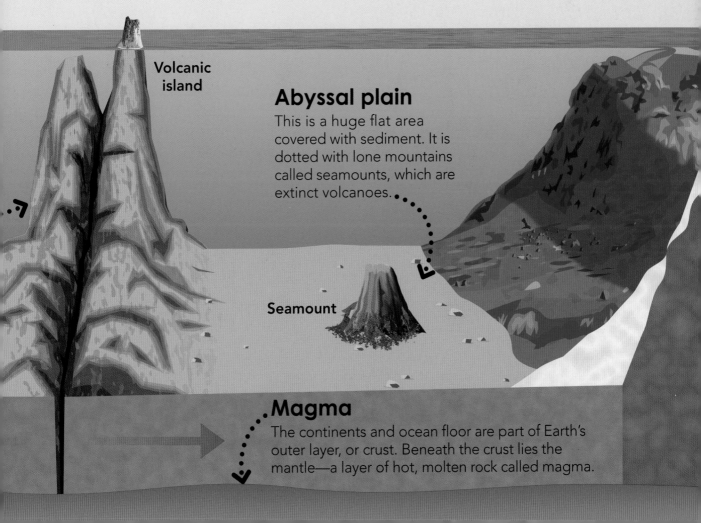

Volcanic island

Abyssal plain

This is a huge flat area covered with sediment. It is dotted with lone mountains called seamounts, which are extinct volcanoes.

Seamount

Magma

The continents and ocean floor are part of Earth's outer layer, or crust. Beneath the crust lies the mantle—a layer of hot, molten rock called magma.

Are there volcanoes underwater?

Yes! Almost two-thirds of all volcanic eruptions happen underwater. New volcanoes form as magma (molten rock) from deep within Earth oozes or bursts out onto the seafloor. The volcanoes grow upward, and some become so tall that they reach the surface.

Vapor

Hot lava vaporizes the water it touches, and volcanic gases are released. In a violent eruption, ash may also be blown out into the water.

The Ring of Fire

A curving chain of more than 450 volcanoes runs 25,000 miles (40,000 km) around the edge of the Pacific Ocean, where tectonic plates meet. The volcanoes are so active that this chain is known as the Ring of Fire.

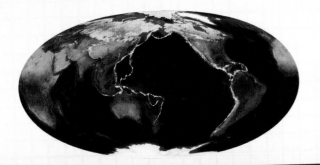

Lava

When hot, glowing magma erupts onto the seabed, it is called lava. The lava's surface cools rapidly and forms a black, glassy skin.

Safe diving

The lava can be about 2,200° F (1,250°C) when it erupts, but it cools so quickly that this diver is safe swimming just above it.

What are the three types of underwater volcano?

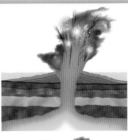

Hot spot

This is when hot magma rises and builds up in one place under the crust. The magma can then burn through to the surface.

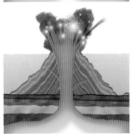

Stratovolcano

This steep-sided volcano is built up from layers of ash and thick lava. The lava cools and hardens before it can spread very far.

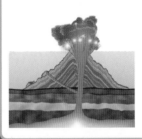

Shield volcano

This type of volcano is less steep than a stratovolcano. It is formed by runny lava that quickly spreads out before it hardens.

Most of the world's volcanic eruptions and earthquakes happen along the Ring of Fire.

? Quick quiz

1. Where is the Ring of Fire?

2. What happens when lava erupts on the seabed?

3. How does a hot spot volcano form?

See pages 132–133 for the answers

Why do icebergs float?

Icebergs float on the ocean because the ice they're made of is less dense, or lighter, than liquid water. Icebergs are also filled with countless tiny air bubbles, which makes them lighter still.

Traveling ice

Icebergs are carried by ocean currents. Eventually, perhaps after many years, they melt and break up when they enter warmer waters.

Breaking away

Large blocks of ice break off glaciers or ice sheets. The blocks tumble into the ocean and drift away as icebergs.

Why does ice float on water?

The water molecules in ice are spaced farther apart than those in liquid water. Ice takes up more space than the same amount of liquid water, making it less dense—so it floats.

Water molecules are close together and move around.

Ice molecules are farther apart and fixed in place.

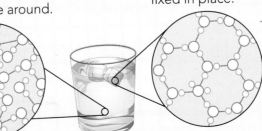

Freshwater ice

Icebergs are made of frozen fresh water. Fresh water is less dense than seawater because it has no salt in it. This makes the icebergs even more buoyant.

Why can you only see the tip of an iceberg?

Ice is only slightly less dense than water, so an iceberg floats low in the water rather than right on top of it. Most of an iceberg is below the surface.

An iceberg called A-76 was larger than the island of Jamaica when it formed in 2021!

? *True or false?*

1. Icebergs are made of fresh water.

2. Fresh water is denser than seawater.

3. The molecules in ice are closer together than those in liquid water.

See pages 132–133 for the answers

How do islands form?

Islands vary in size, from small rocky outcrops to huge areas of land. Most large islands are continental islands—they became separated from the rest of a continent. Oceanic islands are caused by volcanoes that erupt from the seabed.

Can islands sink?

Yes, they can. Volcanic islands are worn down by waves. When volcanoes stop erupting, the ocean floor beneath them cools and shrinks, so they start to sink. Low-lying islands, such as the Hele Islands in the Solomons, shown here, are sinking because their coasts are being eroded and sea levels are rising.

Oceanic islands

Many volcanoes erupt on the deep ocean floor. Occasionally, an underwater volcano grows so big that it creates a new island in the ocean.

? *True or false?*

1. Oceanic islands are formed by volcanoes.

2. Every undersea volcano creates a new island.

3. Rising sea levels can cause islands to sink.

See pages 132–133 for the answers

It can take about 10,000 to 500,000 years for an oceanic island to form.

Continental islands

Some islands form when Earth's continents break apart or when part of a continent is cut off by rising sea levels.

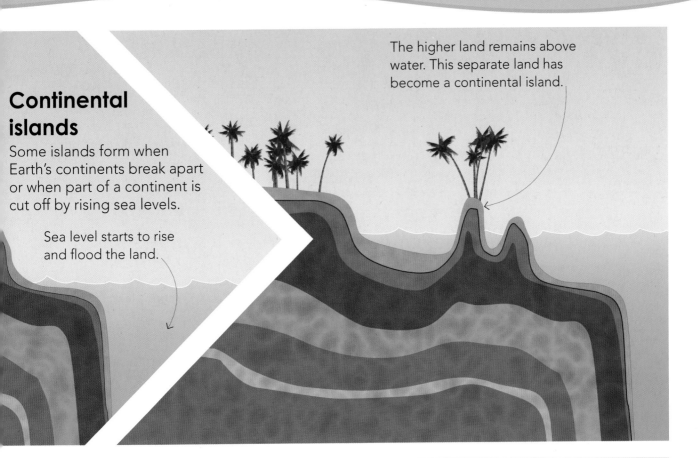

The higher land remains above water. This separate land has become a continental island.

Sea level starts to rise and flood the land.

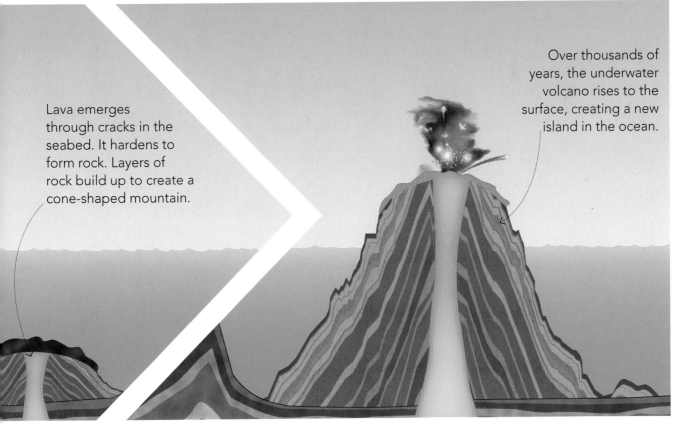

Lava emerges through cracks in the seabed. It hardens to form rock. Layers of rock build up to create a cone-shaped mountain.

Over thousands of years, the underwater volcano rises to the surface, creating a new island in the ocean.

Why are some coasts sandy and others rocky?

Coasts are shaped by the power of the sea. In some places, waves batter cliffs until they collapse into rocky piles. In others, they drop sand or pebbles on the shore to make beaches. Waves can also wash beaches away or pound huge rocks into sand.

Is some sand made from fish poop?

The white sand on many tropical beaches is mostly parrotfish poop! These reef fish crunch dead coral with their parrotlike beaks to eat the algae that live on the coral. They poop out the coral as white grains of sand.

How do sandy coasts form?

Sandy beaches often form in sheltered places, such as estuaries and bays, where the waves have less energy. Here, the sand gradually builds up instead of being washed away.

A sandy beach usually has a gentle slope.

Tiny particles of sand, silt, and clay are washed onto the beach.

Sandy beach

Sand is usually made of fine mineral particles from rocks broken down by the waves or weather. It can also be made of tiny fragments from the shells and skeletons of dead marine life.

Sand can be many different colors—from pale yellow or white to black, red, pink, and even green.

How are rocky coasts shaped?

Softer rock erodes, or gets worn down, quicker than harder rock. So when softer rock between two bits of harder rock gets eroded, it creates an inlet. The force of the waves, chemicals in the water, and pebbles flung against the soft rock gradually wears it away.

Softer rock

Harder rock

Waves

Rocky coast

The rocks can be small fragments, boulders, or rocky shelves and outcrops that extend into the water. Pebbles are rocks worn by the waves into smooth, rounded shapes.

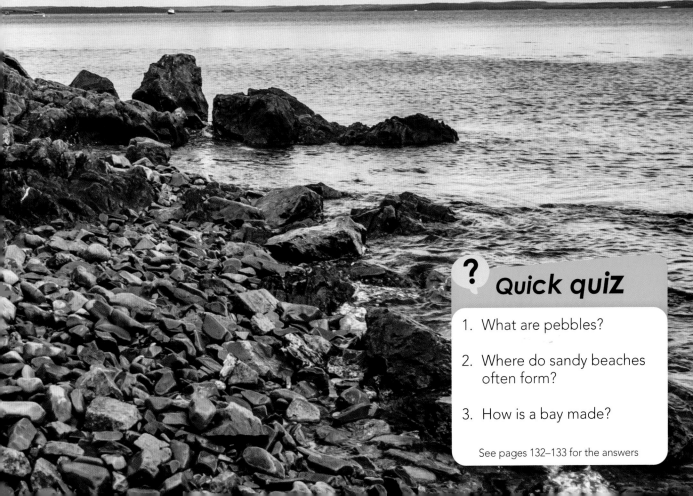

? Quick quiz

1. What are pebbles?

2. Where do sandy beaches often form?

3. How is a bay made?

See pages 132–133 for the answers

Where does sea foam come from?

When the sea is churned by the wind and waves it sometimes produces a whitish froth, called sea foam. The water contains tiny particles and dissolved substances that form bubbles when they get stirred up. Sea foam is usually harmless.

Foamy shore

The tide often carries sea foam onto the shore, where it gets whipped up into a lather, like thick bubble bath.

What's in sea foam?

In addition to water, sea foam contains dissolved salts, proteins, and fats from rotting marine life, dead algae, and sometimes polluting chemicals such as detergents.

Proteins

Salt

Pollutants

Fats

Algae

When is sea foam harmful?

A few types of algae cause health problems if they are present in sea foam. They contain chemicals that can irritate the eyes, nose, and throat of beachgoers, and also kill fish.

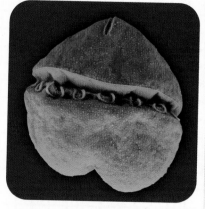

Karenia brevis is a microscopic alga that can cause harmful sea foam.

? Quick quiz

1. What causes a red tide?

2. How does sea foam end up on beaches?

3. What is the usual color of sea foam?

See pages 132–133 for the answers

Is sea foam always white?

Not always, no! Blooms of harmful algae near the shore can turn sea foam red or reddish-brown. This is known as a "red tide." The color comes from a pigment called chlorophyll contained inside the algae.

North American Plate

Eurasian Plate

Separating plates.........

The Mid-Atlantic Ridge is where the North and South American plates pull apart from the Eurasian and African plates. This mid-ocean ridge runs along the floor of the Atlantic.

Does the ocean floor move?

Yes, but only very slowly. Tectonic plates that make up the Earth's crust—including those that make up the ocean floor—are drifting over the planet's surface. At places on the ocean floor called mid-ocean ridges, plates move apart. At other places, called subduction zones, plates crunch together.

Polyp

A coral polyp has a chalky, cup-shaped skeleton that protects its soft body. The polyp catches tiny zooplankton animals with its tentacles and eats them.

Tentacles

Mouth

Gut

Skeleton

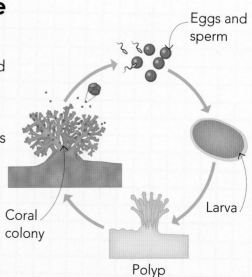

?

Quick quiz

1. What is an individual coral animal called?
   a) a polyp
   b) a platypus
   c) an anemone

2. What is the main cause of coral bleaching?
   a) rising sea temperatures
   b) algae
   c) ocean waves

See pages 132–133 for the answers

Coral life cycle

Coral colonies release eggs and sperm into the water. Each fertilized egg develops into a drifting larva. The larva eventually settles on the seabed and changes into a polyp. From the bottom of each polyp, more polyps sprout to form a colony.

Eggs and sperm

Larva

Polyp

Coral colony

Ocean habitats

The ocean might seem like a vast mass of water, but there are many unique worlds, or habitats, within it. From tiny rock pools to towering kelp forests, every ocean environment presents different challenges to the living things that call it home.

Does grass grow in the ocean?

Yes! Vast underwater meadows of seagrass grow in warm, shallow coastal waters. Seagrass originally grew on land, before it invaded the sea. Like all land plants, seagrass makes its own food. This process is called photosynthesis.

Capturing carbon dioxide

Carbon dioxide (CO_2) in the air dissolves into the ocean. The plants take in dissolved carbon dioxide from the water for photosynthesis.

Using carbon

Seagrass plants use the carbon from carbon dioxide to build new cells for their bodies. The carbon becomes part of the growing plants.

What feeds on seagrass?

Dugong
This marine mammal feeds only on plants. They are sometimes called sea cows because they graze on seagrass meadows.

Sea turtle
The green sea turtle cruises through seagrass meadows. It chomps on grass and seaweed with its saw-edged jaws.

Queen conch
This large sea snail feeds by scraping off the algae that grow on the blades of seagrass. It also nibbles dead seagrass.

Absorbing energy

Sunlight filters down through the shallow water. Seagrass leaves use a chemical called chlorophyll to absorb energy from the sunlight.

Releasing oxygen

When the plants make their food, they release oxygen (O_2) as a waste product. Some oxygen stays dissolved in the ocean. The rest escapes into the air.

? Quick quiz

1. What part of the ocean is seagrass found in?

2. Why are dugongs sometimes called sea cows?

3. What happens to the carbon in seagrass when the plant dies?

See pages 132–133 for the answers

Why is seagrass important?

Seagrass meadows absorb lots of carbon dioxide, one of the gases that cause climate change. When seagrass dies, it gets buried under mud and sand. The carbon inside it is safely trapped in the seabed.

On the seabed

On the move

Sea pen

Looking like an old-fashioned feather quill pen, a sea pen is a colony of tiny animals called polyps.

Sea cucumber

From a small hole in its body, the male sea cucumber ejects sperm into the surrounding water to fertilize a female's eggs.

Frogfish

A frogfish has stumpy fins with broad ends that work like feet to help it grip rocks when it walks over the seabed.

What lives on the seabed?

Bottom-dwelling sea life ranges from seaweeds and barnacles to sponges and sharks. Many living things spend their whole lives anchored to the seabed. Others move over the bottom as they search for food, and some swim or float in the water immediately above.

? True or false?

1. The swell shark inflates its belly with air to deter predators.

2. A sea pen is a fish that lives on the seabed.

3. A frogfish can walk on the seabed.

See pages 132–133 for the answers

Sea slug

Like land slugs, these colorful mollusks use a muscular "foot" and sticky slime to crawl along the seabed.

Burrowing

Tube anemone

These anemones live in feltlike tubes. They wave their tentacles to catch prey and retreat into the tube to escape predators.

Sand striker

This worm burrows into sand, leaving its mouthparts showing. If a fish touches the sensitive antennae, the worm bites!

Are any sharks bottom-dwellers?

Angel shark

These flat-bodied sharks have fins like wings. They lie in the sand and stick their jaws out to snatch fish.

Swell shark

If a predator comes near, the swell shark swallows water to inflate its body and make itself too big to eat.

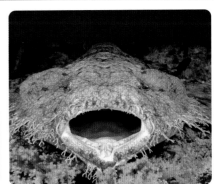

Tasseled wobbegong

A "beard" of skin flaps that look like seaweed helps to disguise the tasseled wobbegong when ambushing prey.

What lives in a rock pool?

Seashore rock pools are little oases of marine life between high and low tide. Seaweeds and algae growing on the rocks provide food for limpets and other plant-eaters. Predators such as starfish and crabs search for meaty meals, while shrimp clear up leftover food scraps.

Seaweed

Pinkish coralline seaweed has a rough, coral-like texture. Most animals don't bother to try eating this gritty seaweed.

Anemone

To stop itself from drying out at low tide, the beadlet anemone pulls its stinging tentacles into its body. This leaves it looking like a blob of red jelly.

Shrimp

Shrimp are the cleaners of the rock pool because they eat the remains of other animals' meals.

Crab

The common shore crab shelters and scavenges for food in rock pools. It hunts shrimp and worms and breaks open mollusk shells with its powerful pincers.

What fish are found in rock pools?

Tiny fish, such as the shanny, make their homes in rock pools. The male shanny guards any eggs laid in the pool by the females, and he chases off would-be egg thieves or rival males that enter his territory.

What type of seaweed is this?
a) sea lettuce
b) coralline seaweed
c) giant kelp

See pages 132–133 for the answer

Light-green sea lettuce grows all year round.

When underwater, the anemone waves its tentacles.

Limpet

Limpets live at the edge of the pool. At high tide, they roam around grazing on algae. When the tide goes out, they clamp their shells firmly onto the rock.

Starfish

The common starfish pulls open mollusks with its tube feet. It pushes its stomach in and dissolves the animal's soft body with digestive juices.

Why are mudflats smelly?

The foul smell from a mudflat comes from bacteria that give off eggy fumes in the thick, gooey mud. Mudflats form when sand and mud carried by rivers or tides settle on the bottom in sheltered places near the shore.

Full of life

Mudflats can only be seen at low tide. They may look empty of life, but the mud itself is teeming with algae, bacteria, and microscopic creatures.

Bacteria

The bacteria feed off decomposing plants and animals trapped in the mud. The bacteria then release hydrogen sulfide gas, which smells like rotten eggs.

Lugworms

The wiggly piles of mud and sand you see on mudflats are the poop of lugworms! As they feed, they eject undigested waste in piles.

Which animals live in the mud?

Cockles, clams, periwinkles, worms, tiny mud shrimp, and fiddler crabs make burrows in the mud. Some sift the mud for edible scraps; others filter food particles from the water when the tide comes in.

Each type of burrowing animal lives at a particular depth in the mud.

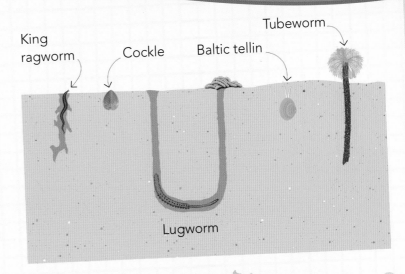

King ragworm

Cockle

Baltic tellin

Tubeworm

Lugworm

Who eats the mudflat burrowers?

Wading birds, such as this sandpiper, probe the mud at low tide in search of prey. At high tide, fish and larger crabs arrive to catch burrowers when they emerge from hiding.

The reeking mudflat gas is the same gas that gives farts their eggy whiff!

? *Quick quiz*

1. What produces the smelly mudflat gas?
   a) algae
   b) bacteria
   c) microscopic animals

2. Which of these does not burrow into the mud?
   a) clam
   b) sandpiper
   c) fiddler crab

See pages 132–133 for the answers

Marshy land

Plants that grow on the marshy land around an estuary need to be able to cope with high levels of salt.

Brackish water

The water near the river mouth is "brackish." This means it is saltier than fresh water, but not as salty as the sea.

Sediment.

Sand and mud dropped at the river mouth slow the waves and absorb their energy. This allows more sand and mud to build up.

What are estuaries?

An estuary is a river mouth, where a river meets the sea. A mixture of mud and sand, called sediment, is laid down in estuaries by rivers and by waves. This creates a range of habitats for wildlife, such as mudflats, salt marshes, and mangroves.

What are salt marshes?

Salt marshes are wetlands that become flooded with salty or brackish water when the tides come in. The grasses and grasslike plants that live there have to survive being partly or completely covered by water.

Extra high spring tide

High tide

Low tide

Spring tide covers nearly all the plants.

River mouth

The less dense (lighter) river water flows out over the seawater. The denser seawater flows underneath it and into the estuary.

What lives in estuaries?

The diamondback terrapin crunches snails, crabs, and clams with its strong jaws. It cries super-salty tears to get rid of salt from its body.

The osprey visits estuaries to hunt fish. This bird of prey swoops down and plucks the fish from the water with its sharp talons.

? Quick quiz

1. Why do ospreys visit estuaries?

2. What is a mix of salty and fresh water called?

3. What happens to salt marsh plants at high tide?

See pages 132–133 for the answers

Why is a coral reef so colorful?

Corals produce colorful, protective pigments when in bright sunlight. Corals also get their colors from tiny algae, called zooxanthellae, that live inside coral polyps. The pigments in the algae shine through the polyps' transparent bodies.

Colorful fish

Bold colors and patterns help fish to find others of their kind on the crowded reef, and to select mates. They can also warn off rivals and predators.

What are the three types of coral reef?

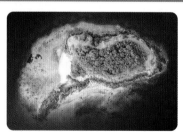

Fringing reef

A fringing reef forms as corals grow in shallow water around an island or along the shoreline of a large landmass.

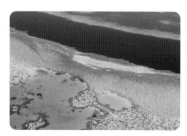

Barrier reef

A barrier reef grows parallel to the shore. The reef is separated from the land by a large lagoon of open water.

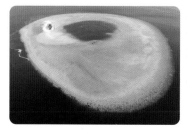

Atoll

An atoll is a coral ring around a lagoon. It forms when a volcanic island sinks but the fringing reef around it keeps growing.

? Quick quiz

1. What is a circular coral reef called?

2. Which type of coral builds the reef—hard or soft?

3. What are zooxanthellae?

See pages 132–133 for the answers

Hard coral

Hard corals are the reef builders. Their polyps have stiff, chalky skeletons. The reef builds up as new polyps grow on the skeletons of dead ones.

Soft coral

The polyps of soft corals do not have skeletons, but they do grow on reefs. Colonies of soft corals often have a treelike or bushy shape.

Camouflage

Colors stand out in the clear reef water. The color of these reef fish match the bright pinks and oranges of the corals.

Zooxanthellae

These algae make sugary food by photosynthesis. They share this food with the polyps. In return, the polyps provide the algae with a safe place to live and supply them with carbon dioxide to carry out photosynthesis.

What are the hottest parts of the ocean?

Hydrothermal vents are the hottest parts of the ocean. Here, jets of scalding water full of dissolved minerals spurt through cracks in the seabed. In complete darkness, these minerals help to support a food chain of bacteria and animals, including odd-looking worms and crabs.

What lives around hydrothermal vents?

Giant tubeworms
Red-gilled tubeworms nearly 6 ft (2 m) long cluster around the chimneys. Bacteria living inside the worms supply them with food.

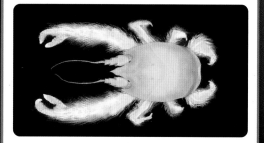

Yeti crab
This crab is known for its long hairs that look like fur. It is named after the Yeti—the legendary furry creature said to live in the Himalayas in Asia.

Mineral jet
As the hot jet mixes with cold ocean water, some of the dissolved minerals turn solid. They settle on the seabed or build up to form tall "chimneys."

Heating up
Cold water seeps down through cracks in the seabed. The water gets heated by magma below the surface and dissolves minerals from rocks.

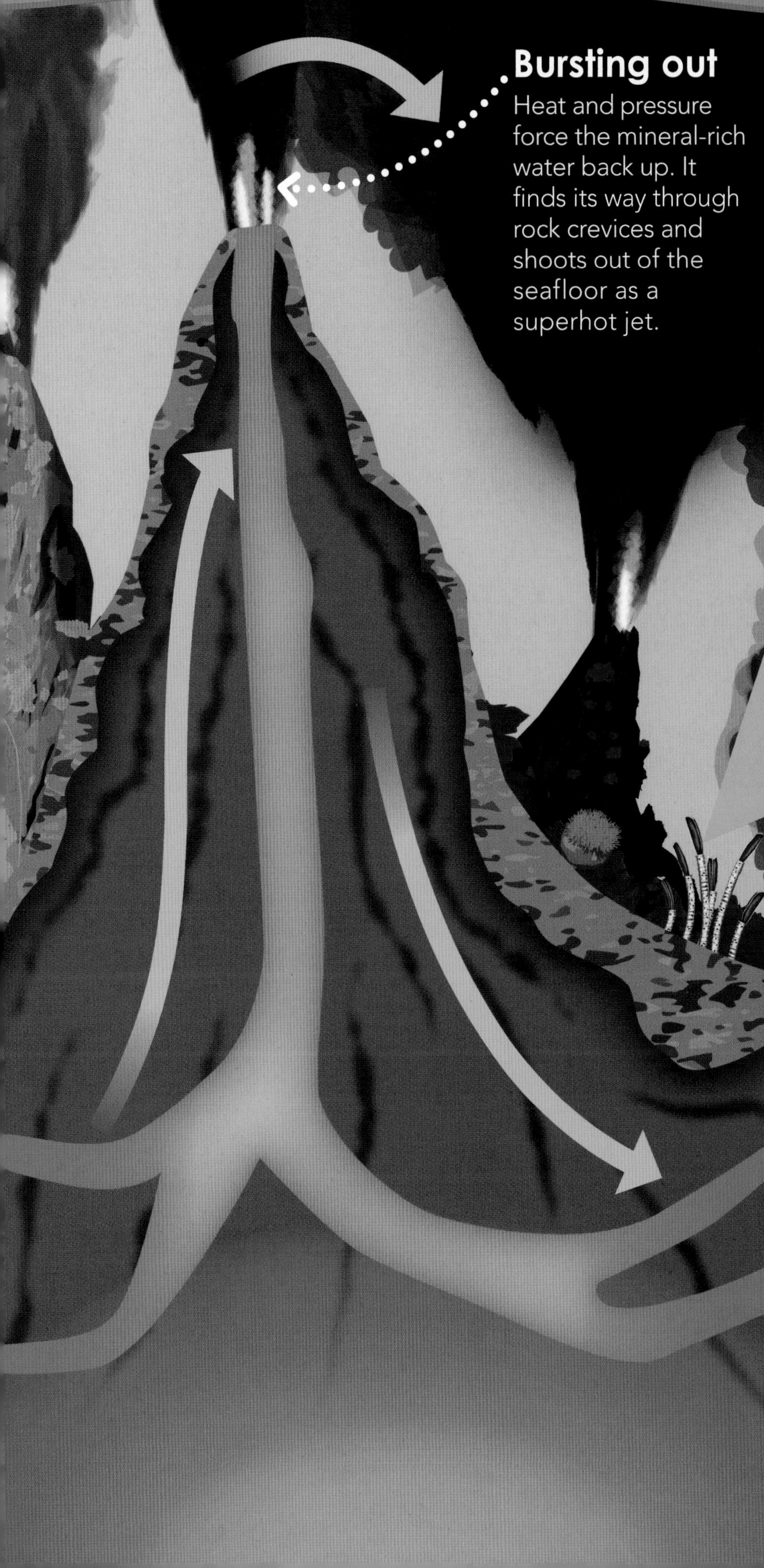

Bursting out

Heat and pressure force the mineral-rich water back up. It finds its way through rock crevices and shoots out of the seafloor as a superhot jet.

Tiny organisms called microbes, which include bacteria, use the minerals in the jets to make their food. The microbes also provide food for other animals that live around the vents.

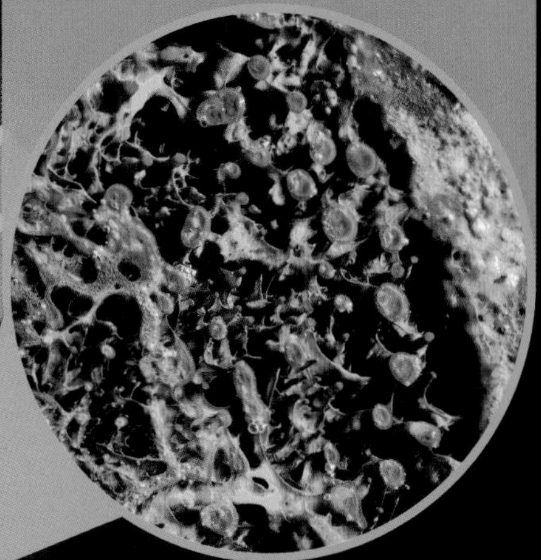

? Quick quiz

1. What heats the cold water that seeps down through the seabed?

2. Does sunlight fuel life around a vent?

3. What is in the hot water that shoots out of a vent?

See pages 132–133 for the answers

Can trees grow in salty water?

Forests of mangrove trees grow along muddy coasts in many tropical regions of the world. Unlike other trees, mangroves can cope with the high levels of salt in seawater. Many marine animals find shelter and food in the shallows among the mangrove roots.

What lives among mangrove roots?

Fiddler crab
At low tide, fiddler crabs emerge from their burrows to feed. Males wave their single large claw to attract females.

Mudskipper
This fish can survive out of water! To help it breathe, it absorbs oxygen through its moist skin. It crawls over the mud on its fins and climbs mangrove roots.

Saltwater crocodile
This is the world's largest crocodile. It visits mangrove forests to hunt for prey sheltering among the roots.

Stilt roots
Stiltlike roots grow out from the trunk and curve down into the mud. The roots collect oxygen from the air, spread the tree's weight, and anchor it in place.

Mangroves filter salt from the water as it enters their roots. Some get rid of salt through their leaves. The salt forms crystals on the surface of the leaves.

? Quick quiz

1. Where do mangrove forests grow?

2. What is the world's biggest crocodile called?

3. How does the mudskipper survive out of water?

See pages 132–133 for the answers

Snorkel roots

Some mangroves have roots that lie under the mud. The snorkel-like root tips poke up through the mud and collect oxygen from the air at low tide.

Why don't polar animals freeze?

Warm-blooded polar animals, such as orcas and penguins, have a layer of fat called blubber that keeps their bodies warm in the icy seas around the North and South poles. Cold-blooded polar fish often have chemicals in their bodies that stop them from turning to blocks of ice.

Emperor penguin
Blood flowing to a penguin's feet is kept cooler than the rest of the bird's blood, so that the bare feet lose less heat to the water and ice.

Arctic bowhead whales have blubber up to 20 in (50 cm) thick.

Crocodile icefish
These fish have snouts a bit like a crocodile. They produce "antifreeze" chemicals that stop their blood from freezing solid.

Polar bear

Waterproof fur helps protect polar bears as they swim. Small ears and a short tail reduce the area from which body heat can escape.

What is blubber?

Dermis, the thickest layer of the skin

Epidermis, the skin's outer layer

Blubber (fat)

Connective tissue

Blubber is a fatty layer that traps body heat and protects many polar animals from the cold. It also stores energy that the animal can use when food is scarce.

Bearded seal

Like all seals, the bearded seal has a thick layer of blubber under its skin. This helps it stay warm in the water and when resting on sea ice.

Orca

Orcas are warm-blooded mammals. They generate heat inside their bodies that helps them keep a stable temperature.

? Quick quiz

1. Why doesn't an icefish's blood turn to ice?

2. Is an orca a fish or a mammal?

3. How thick is the blubber of the Arctic bowhead whale?

See pages 132–133 for the answers

Do flowers grow in the ocean?

Yes, they do, but most people never see them! Almost all the things in the ocean that seem to be flowers are actually invertebrates—animals without backbones. What look like colorful petals are often body parts that the animal uses to feed.

The spines break off in a predator's skin.

Prickly plant?

Is this a thistle? No, it's a sea urchin, covered with protective spines that resemble prickly leaves. Some urchins have venomous spines.

Deadly colors

These trumpet-shaped "flowers" are zoanthids—relatives of corals and anemones. The bright colors of many zoanthids warn that they are poisonous.

Zoanthid polyps grow in colonies.

Fertilized flowers produce seeds.

The gills take in oxygen and filter food from the sea.

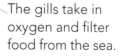

Spiral patterns

The gills of the Christmas tree worm look like flower whorls. The rest of the worm's body lies buried in the seabed in a tube.

Why don't algae produce flowers?

Marine algae are not true plants. Instead of growing flowers that produce seeds, they release microscopic spores from their leaflike blades. The male spores fertilize the female spores to make new algae.

The arms pass food to the mouth.

The tentacles kill prey and deter enemies.

Frilly feeder

The bright and bushy feather star is an animal with up to 200 frilly arms. It extends the arms to feed, and the currents cause them to "wave" in the water.

Coral

Flowerpot corals look like a cluster of potted flowers. Each of their daisylike polyps has 24 stinging tentacles around its mouth.

True flower

Seagrasses are the only plants that flower under the ocean. Male flowers release pollen into the water. The pollen fertilizes the female flowers.

? Quick quiz

1. Which of these produces the only ocean flower?
   a) sea urchin
   b) seagrass
   c) zoanthid

2. What do algae release into the water to reproduce?
   a) spores
   b) pollen
   c) seeds

See pages 132–133 for the answers

Are there forests in the ocean?

Vast "forests" do indeed flourish in cold coastal waters. However, although they are called forests, there are no trees in them! They are made up of giant kelp seaweed, which is not a plant, but a type of algae. Giant kelp forests provide shelter for fish and other ocean animals.

Green sea turtle

Kelp bass

Sunflower star

Do some fish migrate to the shore?

Some fish live permanently near the shore, but others are occasional visitors. Certain fish of the open ocean, such as sardines and anchovies, arrive in great schools to feed on the plankton that live in coastal waters.

Forest floor life

Sea urchins, brittle stars, and snails graze on kelp tendrils. Sea cucumbers feed on rotting kelp scraps, while sunflower starfish prey on sea cucumbers, urchins, and snails.

Kelp forest

Giant kelp forests tower 100 ft (30 m) or more above the seabed. The kelp is anchored to the bottom by tendrils called holdfasts. Giant kelp can grow by 18 in (45 cm) in a day.

Kelp rockfish

Leopard shark

Gorgonian sea fan

Forest swimmers

Seals and sea lions weave through the kelp as they hunt for fish. Sea otters shelter here from storms and sharks. The otters are good for the forest, because they eat the urchins that attack the kelp.

Sea otter

? Quick quiz

1. Is giant kelp a type of ocean plant?

2. Why do sardine schools arrive at the coast?

3. What keeps giant kelp anchored to the seabed?

See pages 132–133 for the answers

Ocean life

The sea is home to a mind-boggling array of living things, from the microscopic algae and animals that make up plankton to the enormous whales and sharks that are the top ocean predators. The sun's energy makes marine life possible, just as it does life on land.

How does sunlight power ocean life?

Marine plants and algae use energy from sunlight to make food and grow. The energy passes on to animals that eat them, and then to predators that eat those animals. The way energy moves between living things is called a food chain.

Sun

Light is a form of energy. You can feel the warming power of sunlight on your skin on a sunny day.

Apex predator

At the top of the food chain is a predator that has no enemies. It is called the apex predator.

Orcas are the apex predator of this food chain—they eat seals, but no other animal in the wild preys on orcas.

Leopard seals hunt lots of animals, including birds and mammals as well as fish.

Large fish

The small fish, in turn, are eaten by bigger fish—and so these large fish gain their energy.

Antarctic toothfish prey on silverfish.

Mammals

The big fish may themselves get eaten by larger predators, such as seals.

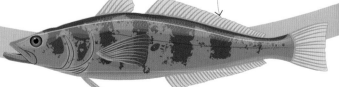

Dinoflagellates are a type of microscopic algae.

Phytoplankton

Microscopic algae called phytoplankton use energy from sunlight to make their own food by a process called photosynthesis.

Zooplankton includes shrimplike krill.

Zooplankton

Tiny creatures called zooplankton eat the algae and absorb their energy.

Antarctic silverfish gulp down vast numbers of krill.

Small fish

Zooplankton provide food and energy for small fish. This makes energy move up the food chain.

Are all fish carnivores?

No! Some reef fish, such as tangs, blennies, and parrotfish, graze on algae. These fish stop the coral from becoming overgrown with algae. Other fish eat both algae and small animals.

Yellow tang

Bicolor blenny

? Quick quiz

1. Which animals prey on orcas in the wild?

2. Does the yellow tang eat algae?

3. What is the passing of food and energy from one living thing to another called?

See pages 132–133 for the answers

Big fish

At 40 ft (12 m) long, the whale shark is the biggest fish. This gentle giant swims with its mouth open, straining zooplankton, small fish, and squid from the water.

Upthrust

The water pushes back up on the whale shark's body with a force called upthrust. The larger the animal, the more upthrust there is to support it.

Why do the biggest animals live in the ocean?

Water is denser than air, so it supports bodies better. That's why animals in the ocean can grow so big. When washed ashore, whales, sharks, and gigantic squid are helpless and floppy without water to hold them up.

The colossal squid has eyes the size of soccer balls—the largest eyes in the animal world.

The largest animal ever

The blue whale is the biggest animal that has ever lived. It is slightly longer, and three times heavier, than Dreadnoughtus, one of the largest of the dinosaurs.

30 African elephants

Blue whale, 100 ft (30 m)

10 African elephants

Dreadnoughtus, 85 ft (26 m)

Body support

A whale shark's body is supported by a skeleton made of rubbery cartilage. Cartilage is strong, but much lighter than bone, and is also very flexible.

How colossal is a colossal squid?

This squid grows to about 46 ft (14 m) long. It is the largest of all invertebrates (animals without a backbone). Colossal squid live in the ocean around Antarctica, where they hunt fish and other squid.

? Quick quiz

1. Why do big ocean animals become floppy when washed ashore?

2. What type of animal is the colossal squid?

3. Was the Dreadnoughtus larger than the blue whale?

See pages 132–133 for the answers

Giant cuttlefish

A cuttlefish can change its color and texture instantly to match its surroundings. It then becomes almost invisible against coral, rock, or sand.

Mimic octopus

This copycat scares off predators by mimicking the colors, shapes, and movements of venomous creatures, such as sea snakes, lionfish, and jellyfish.

How do sea animals use camouflage?

Some sea animals use color or shape to blend into the background or disguise themselves as other things. This is called camouflage. It can help these animals hide from hungry hunters or sneak up on unwary prey.

The stonefish opens its mouth and sucks in prey in less than a second!

Leafy sea dragon

The leaflike flaps on the sea dragon's body help conceal it among seaweed fronds and seagrass blades. Leafy sea dragons are close cousins of seahorses.

Stonefish

With its craggy, mottled skin, this fish is hard to spot among stones, rocks, and reefs. It lies perfectly still until a fish swims close enough for it to gulp down in a flash.

How do decorator crabs stay safe?

To mask their appearance, decorator crabs cover themselves with objects that they find on the seabed. They attach snippets of seaweed, small shells and stones, and even animals, such as sponges, to the hooklike hairs on their bodies.

? True or false?

1. Decorator crabs decorate the seafloor with shells.

2. Leafy sea dragons are related to seahorses.

3. Stonefish are very slow eaters.

See pages 132–133 for the answers

Are octopuses really brainy?

Octopuses are among the smartest of all invertebrates. They use tools and solve problems, such as unscrewing a jam-jar lid. Octopuses are also great at adapting to different habitats and escaping or fighting off predators.

Do fish ever use tools?

Yes! Tuskfish smash clams against hard coral to break the shells so they can eat the clams inside. When animals make use of objects around them, they are called tool-users.

Veined octopus

This octopus collects empty clam shells to hide in! It pulls two half-shells around its body to protect itself from hungry predators.

Big brain

Although it has eight other brains, the octopus is mainly controlled by a central, doughnut-shaped brain inside its head.

Suckers

Each arm has two rows of muscly suckers that can grip prey and other objects. The suckers can also taste and touch things.

? True or false?

1. Octopuses can unscrew the lids of jam jars.

2. Octopuses have eight brains.

3. The veined octopus collects shells with the clams inside.

See pages 132–133 for the answers

Which crab uses shells to hide in?

The rear part of a young coconut crab's body is soft, so the crab hides in an old seashell for protection. The crab discards the shell once a hard covering has formed over its abdomen.

Brainy arms

An octopus has a tiny brain in every arm. Each arm can move on its own without being told what to do by the main brain.

Can fish see in the dark?

Many fish in the deep, dark midnight zone are blind. However, in the twilight zone, where a little light reaches, most fish can see. Some fish have big eyes to gather as much light as possible. Those with small, weak eyes rely on other senses, such as smell.

Barreleye fish

The tube-shaped eyes of this fish are great at collecting light in the dim water. The front of the head is see-through, to let as much light as possible reach the eyes.

How do ocean animals hide from big-eyed predators?

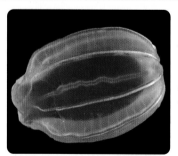

Red comb jelly

Red light does not reach the deep ocean, so red is a good camouflage color in the depths. To other deep-sea creatures, whose eyes can only see blue, this red comb jelly looks black.

Hatchetfish

The body of a hatchetfish is so slim that it is hard to spot from below. Light organs along its belly break up the fish's silhouette when seen against the brighter water above.

? True or false?

1. Deep-sea animals use electricity to flash and glow with light.

2. Red is the only color that is visible in the deep ocean.

3. Many deep-sea fish are blind.

See pages 132–133 for the answers

Dark back

The darker color of the barreleye's back hides it against the murky depths when looked at from above.

Eyes

The fish points its tube-shaped eyes upward, searching for food overhead. The eyes swivel forward as the fish darts up to snatch prey.

"Bioluminescence" means "light from living things."

Silvery scales

Shiny scales on its body give this fish the nickname "mirror belly." The silvery scales reflect light away from the eyes of predators and prey.

What is bioluminescence?

Bioluminescence is the way that many animals flash or glow with light to confuse predators, lure prey, or attract mates. Their bodies contain pockets of bacteria that make light from chemicals.

Deep-sea anglerfish

What are the biggest ocean predators?

The largest predators at sea include whales, fast-swimming sharks, and intelligent dolphins. Some cruise the surface waters in search of prey. Others look for food down in the murky depths of the ocean.

Orcas are the only natural enemies of great white sharks.

Orcas live and hunt in family groups called pods.

Sperm whale
This bus-sized hunter dives down more than 1.2 miles (2 km) to feed on deep-water squid. It can hold its breath for 90 minutes.

The huge head houses the largest brain of any animal.

What other deadly creatures live in the ocean?

Blue-ringed octopus

The vivid blue rings on this octopus warn that it has a venomous bite. Its toxic saliva is powerful enough to kill a human.

Pufferfish

The body of a pufferfish contains a lethal poison. When threatened, the fish puffs itself up into a prickly ball to deter predators.

? Quick quiz

1. Which hunter has the biggest animal brain of all?

2. How many teeth does a great white shark have?

3. What is a group of orcas called?

See pages 132–133 for the answers

The muscle-packed body gives the shark a top speed of 35 mph (56 kph).

Orcas

A type of dolphin, orcas are clever mammals. They team up to knock seals off ice floes and form packs to kill whales bigger than themselves.

Great white shark

The great white has powerful jaws lined with 300 razor-sharp, serrated teeth. This lone predator hunts seals, dolphins, large fish, and even whales.

Do fish migrate like birds?

A European eel can take a year to swim from its river home out to the Sargasso Sea!

Sometimes, yes. There are fish that make long journeys to find the best places to feed or to spawn (breed). These migrations are usually circular trips at sea. However, a few fish leave the sea to spawn in freshwater rivers, while others swim out of rivers to breed in the salty ocean.

Salmon swim from the ocean to rivers.

Sockeye salmon

After living as adults in the Pacific Ocean, sockeye salmon swim up North American rivers, jumping rapids as they go. They die soon after spawning. The new, young fish then head out to sea when they are old enough.

Young fish head back to sea.

PACIFIC OCEAN

Adult eels swim to the Sargasso Sea.

How do fish navigate?

Scientists think that sharks, salmon, and other migrating fish find their way in the open sea by sensing Earth's magnetic field. Their keen sense of smell may also help when they are closer to shore.

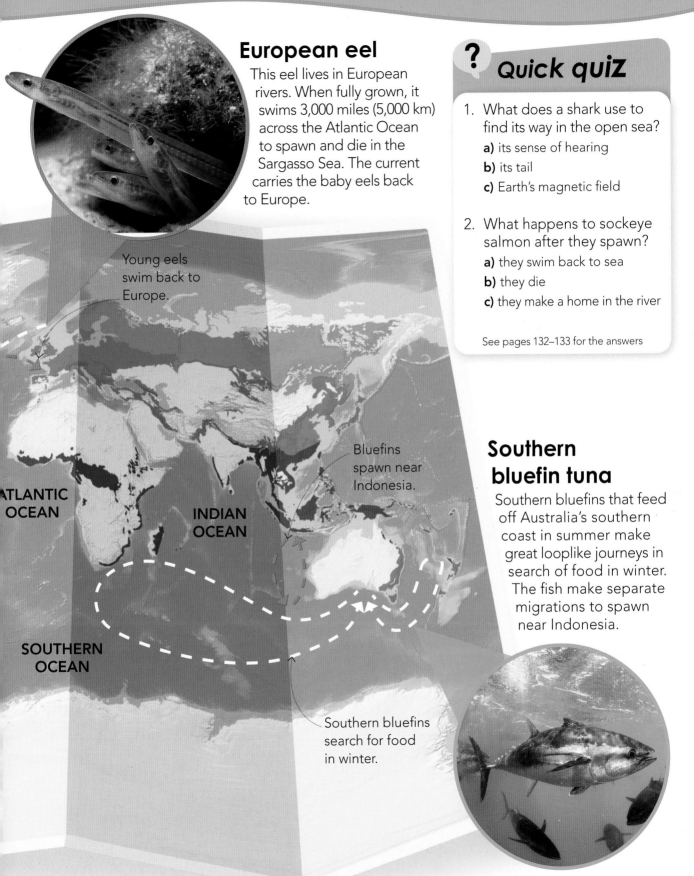

European eel

This eel lives in European rivers. When fully grown, it swims 3,000 miles (5,000 km) across the Atlantic Ocean to spawn and die in the Sargasso Sea. The current carries the baby eels back to Europe.

Young eels swim back to Europe.

ATLANTIC OCEAN

INDIAN OCEAN

SOUTHERN OCEAN

Bluefins spawn near Indonesia.

Southern bluefins search for food in winter.

? Quick quiz

1. What does a shark use to find its way in the open sea?
   a) its sense of hearing
   b) its tail
   c) Earth's magnetic field

2. What happens to sockeye salmon after they spawn?
   a) they swim back to sea
   b) they die
   c) they make a home in the river

See pages 132–133 for the answers

Southern bluefin tuna

Southern bluefins that feed off Australia's southern coast in summer make great looplike journeys in search of food in winter. The fish make separate migrations to spawn near Indonesia.

Sea pig

A sea pig is a deep-ocean sea cucumber. It has a pink-tinged, see-through body. The sea pig crawls over the mud on its tube feet looking for tasty morsels.

Dumbo octopus

The dumbo octopus flaps a pair of earlike fins on its head to push itself through the water. It steers with its eight arms.

Tripod fish

The tripod fish has long rays sticking out from its fins, which look like antennae and can be used to detect prey. It also uses them to stand on.

Deep-sea sea pen

What lives in the ocean depths?

The deep ocean floor is covered by soft mud, called ooze. The ooze is the rotting remains of dead sea life that have drifted down through the water above. Many bottom-dwelling animals sift the ooze for edible scraps. Predators hunt these seabed scavengers.

? Quick quiz

1. How does a dumbo octopus move through the water?

2. What type of animal is a sea pig?

3. How does a grenadier fish detect prey in the ooze?

See pages 132–133 for the answers

Giant sea spider

This spiderlike creature walks over the seafloor on long spindly legs. It uses its tubelike mouth to suck the insides out of its prey.

Abyssal grenadier

As the grenadier swims just above the seabed, the fleshy barbels on its chin sense prey wriggling in the ooze. It can also smell a meal of rotting flesh from afar.

Basket star

Trench life

At the bottom of ocean trenches, the deepest places of all, the pressure can be 1,000 times greater than at the surface. Amazingly, some animals thrive here. They include fish, such as cusk eels and snailfish, and shrimplike giant amphipods up to 12 in (30 cm) long.

Giant amphipod

Abyssal cusk eel

Mariana snailfish

Why are some fish flabby out of water?

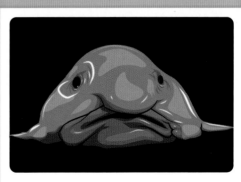

Deep-sea fish, such as blobfish, survive the huge pressures by having lots of water in their body tissues. When they are brought to the surface, where the pressure is much lower, their soft bodies swell up and lose their shape.

How fast can fish swim?

The swiftest swimmer in the ocean is the sailfish, which can match the fastest jet-ski for pace. Speedsters like the sailfish swim slowly most of the time, and only increase their speed to chase down the fastest prey.

Which fish is the slowest?

The slowest-swimming fish may be the dwarf seahorse, whose top speed is just 5 ft (1.5 m) per hour. Like all seahorses, it swims upright, using its flickering dorsal fin to propel it.

Blue shark
Blue, slender, and graceful, this shark is also fast. It is capable of bursts of speed reaching 43 mph (69 kph).

Bluefin tuna
Bluefins often cruise at a leisurely pace, but these torpedo-shaped hunters can notch 43 mph (70 kph) when they need to.

How do fish float in water?

Many fish have an air-filled bag called a swim bladder inside their bodies. The swim bladder helps them float in midwater instead of sinking to the bottom. By letting gas in or out of the swim bladder, they can rise or sink in the water.

Gas moves in and out of the bladder to help keep the fish level in the water.

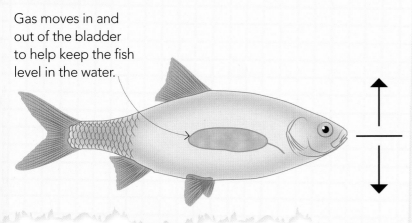

? Quick quiz

1. Which fish is the fastest?
   a) shortfin mako shark
   b) blue shark
   c) bluefin tuna

2. What does a swim bladder do?
   a) helps a fish to swim faster
   b) keeps the fish clean
   c) helps a fish float in midwater

See pages 132–133 for the answers

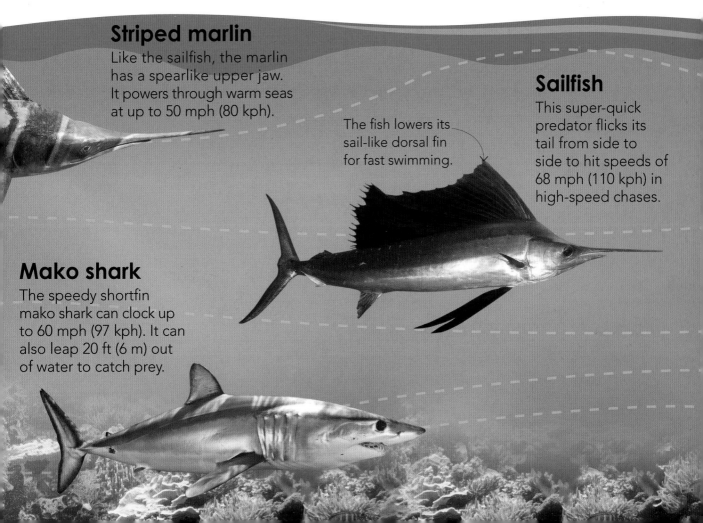

Striped marlin

Like the sailfish, the marlin has a spearlike upper jaw. It powers through warm seas at up to 50 mph (80 kph).

The fish lowers its sail-like dorsal fin for fast swimming.

Sailfish

This super-quick predator flicks its tail from side to side to hit speeds of 68 mph (110 kph) in high-speed chases.

Mako shark

The speedy shortfin mako shark can clock up to 60 mph (97 kph). It can also leap 20 ft (6 m) out of water to catch prey.

Why do dolphins leap?

Dolphins leap to help them travel faster. This is because there is less drag (friction) when moving through air than through water. Leaping also helps them see farther and to take in the extra air they need for speedy swimming. Dolphins may make vertical jumps as a way of signaling to each other—or they may just do it for fun!

Dorsal fin

The fin on a dolphin's back is called the dorsal fin. It keeps the animal upright in the water, so that its body doesn't roll from side to side.

Eye spy

Leaping helps dolphins hunt for prey. They may spot seabirds in the distance feeding on fish schools. Viewing the coastline can help them navigate.

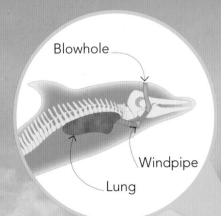

Blowhole

Windpipe

Lung

Blowhole

When they surface, dolphins breathe through a blowhole (opening) on top of their heads. The blowhole closes when they dive.

Flipper

The "flippers," or pectoral fins, are used for steering, balancing, and stopping. They don't push the dolphin through the water.

Does a flying fish really fly?

Yes, and no! Unlike birds, flying fish aren't capable of powered, flapping flight. However, they can glide. To escape danger, they leap from the water and sail through the air on their outstretched fins for up to 50 ft (15 m).

Do sharks jump?

Yes, some sharks jump. Great whites make spectacular leaps, called breaching, to catch fast-moving prey. Spinner sharks burst from the water with their bodies spinning as they swim upward through schools of fish.

Great white breaching

? Picture quiz

Which animal is leaping out of the water onto sea ice?

See pages 132–133 for the answer

Shaped for speed

A tapering, torpedo-shaped body, swept-back fins, and smooth skin all help the dolphin to cut through the water easily.

Tail

A dolphin swims by swishing its tail up and down. Muscles along the dolphin's back and sides beat the tail powerfully.

Sleeping bag

This parrotfish has sealed itself into a "sleeping bag" made of mucus secreted from its mouth. The gooey covering keeps bloodsucking parasites away from the fish while it rests.

Do fish sleep?

Many fish have a resting time when they don't respond to things around them—just like we do when we fall asleep. These sleeping fish float in midwater or hide in a safe place. However, other fish keep moving and never seem to sleep at all.

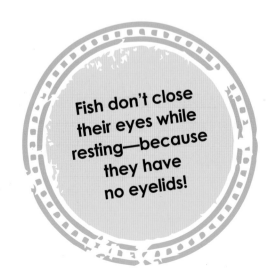

Fish don't close their eyes while resting—because they have no eyelids!

Buried at bedtime

The sand lance wriggles its body down into the sandy seabed when it's time for bed! Lying buried and unseen, the fish rests and saves its energy until it emerges again to feed.

Seabed snooze

Many sharks swim nonstop to keep their gills working. However, some, including the Port Jackson shark, can rest on the bottom. It opens and closes its mouth to pump water over its gills.

Safe hiding place

When resting on the reef, a triggerfish wedges itself between coral branches. It raises the spines on its back to lock itself tightly in place, so predators can't drag it out.

Why do dolphins sleep with one eye open?

Only one half of a dolphin's brain sleeps at a time. The other half stays awake so the dolphin can keep breathing, and one eye remains open to watch out for threats. When the brain's right half sleeps, the left eye shuts. The right eye closes when the brain's left half rests.

? Quick quiz

1. Can a dolphin breathe while it's asleep?

2. Which fish hides in the sand to rest?

3. Why does a resting parrotfish cover itself in gooey mucus?

See pages 132–133 for the answers

How do birds survive at sea?

The ocean is a rich feeding ground for birds. Some seabirds, such as the albatross, spend most of their lives on the open sea. Other birds make short flights over the ocean to feed, launching themselves off clifftops or rocky perches.

Albatross
This magnificent seabird only comes to land to breed. It eats mostly squid, snatching them just below the surface.

How do seabirds find their way?

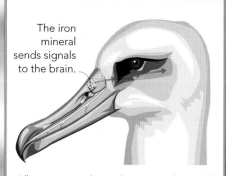

The iron mineral sends signals to the brain.

Albatrosses and petrels navigate by smell and by following Earth's magnetic field. Their beaks contain an iron mineral that responds to Earth's changing magnetism as they fly over the surface.

Wings
The albatross stretches out its long, stiff wings to soar effortlessly on the wind. The wing bones lock straight at the elbow.

Webbed feet
The bird paddles with its feet when it settles on the water to feed. It takes off by running over the surface and flapping its wings.

Soaring flight

An albatross can stay airborne for a long time by soaring up into the wind, then gliding back down to the sea. This type of flying uses very little energy, because the bird only occasionally needs to flap its wings.

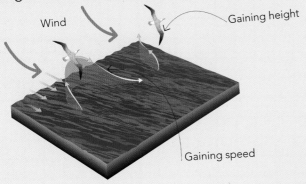

Wind

Gaining height

Gaining speed

To find food for their chicks, albatrosses can travel 1,600 miles (2,600 km) from their nests.

Feathers

The feathers keep the albatross warm and dry. Like all birds, the albatross uses its beak to clean its feathers and coat them with a protective oil. This is called preening.

Nostrils

The albatross has tube-shaped nostrils on its beak. These funnel scents and help the bird smell squid a long way off.

? Picture quiz

What do you think this puffin is doing to its feathers?

See pages 132–133 for the answer

What happens to sea animals when they die?

When an ocean creature dies, it sinks. Most are eaten on the way down, but some reach the seabed and provide food for animals that live on the ocean floor. A large animal carcass, such as a dead whale, can feed a host of living things for years.

What is marine snow?

Marine snow is the nonstop shower of rotting material from dead marine organisms that falls to the seafloor. Deep-sea life depends on marine snow for food.

All sorts of sea creatures join the feast—including hagfish and shrimp.

Flesh-eaters

Within hours of a dead whale coming to rest on the bottom, sharks and other flesh-eating fish arrive. They eat the whale's blubber, muscle, and internal organs.

Scrap scavengers

Squat lobsters, bristleworms, and other small animals arrive to feed on the slowly disintegrating body of the whale. Some worms feed on whale oil soaked into the seabed.

How do fish fossils form?

Fossils form when fish bodies get buried in tiny particles called sediment. This gradually turns to rock over thousands of years. Only the hard parts of a fish's body fossilize—the soft parts quickly rot away.

? Quick quiz

1. Which arrives at a whale carcass first—a tubeworm or a zombie worm?

2. Do all dead animals end up on the ocean floor?

3. Which parts of a fish's body can get fossilized—the soft or hard parts?

See pages 132–133 for the answers

At any one time there are around 700,000 dead whales on the ocean floor.

The bacteria that remain support a rich variety of sea life, including mussels, tubeworms, clams, and limpets.

A pink fuzz of bone-eating zombie worms covers the skeleton.

Bacteria banquet

Soon, only the skeleton of the whale is left. Bacteria digest the bones, and their waste provides fuel for other bacteria growing nearby.

Do sea serpents exist?

Yes, and no! Certainly, there are snakes that swim in the ocean. Long ago, sailors told tales of sea monsters. Their stories may have been based on sea snakes, giant squid, and other real-life creatures of the deep.

Frilled shark

This predator shark is a scary sight! It has wide jaws lined with needle-sharp teeth. Each tooth is shaped like a trident—with three prongs. Its snake-like body can reach up to 6½ ft (2 m) long.

Giant oarfish

This deep-water fish is rarely seen at the surface and can reach an amazing 26 ft (8 m) in length. However, this huge creature is actually a harmless plankton-eater that lacks real teeth and scales.

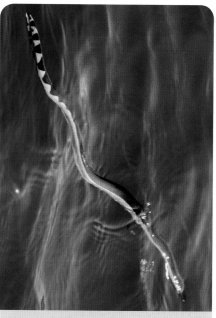

Sea snake

The yellow-bellied sea snake lives its whole life at sea, never coming ashore. It has a powerful venom, but it is only about 3 ft (1 m) long— perhaps not big enough to frighten tough sailors?

Mythical monsters

Sailors once told stories of sea serpents that terrorized their ships. The creatures were said to have incredibly long bodies that could rear out of the water and coil up around masts before gobbling up sailors for their dinner.

Is the Kraken real?

The Kraken is a legendary sea monster from Norse mythology, believed to have been based on the giant squid. However, at up to 40 ft (13 m) long, the giant squid is not as huge as the Kraken and would not be big enough to overwhelm a ship!

Oceans and us

The ocean gives us food, minerals, energy, and so much more. Most of the ocean is still unexplored, and there is always something new to find out. What we do know is that human activities are changing the oceans and harming the life that lives within them.

Energy

The seafloor holds great stores of oil and gas. We can also get energy from the waves and tides, and from the wind by using wind turbines like these.

Food

Fish and other seafood are a rich source of protein and other nutrients. Worldwide, around 60 million people work in the fishing and fish-farming industries.

Rocks and minerals

We get salt from the ocean by evaporating seawater. Sand and gravel from beaches are used for building. There are also valuable metals locked up in the seabed.

How do oceans help us?

Oceans are essential to how we live. They help regulate our climate and provide us with food, energy, minerals, jobs, and leisure activities. Moving goods by sea is cheaper and less harmful to the environment than moving them by air.

Around 80 percent of all the world's goods are transported by sea.

Living by the sea

The sea provides food and the chance to travel and trade. Many cities have been built along the coast and near estuaries, where rivers meet the ocean.

Sports and leisure

Ocean activities include sailing, surfing, swimming, snorkeling, and scuba-diving. Jet-skis and powerboats offer thrills for some, while others prefer a lazy day at the beach!

Trade and travel

Container ships and tankers deliver cargo and fuel around the world. Ferries carry passengers across narrow seas, and cruise ships take tourists on ocean vacations.

What are cables along the ocean floor used for?

Communication cables on the seabed send telephone and internet signals between different continents and countries. Some cables run for many thousands of miles. There are also ocean-floor cables that carry electricity and underwater pipes that deliver oil, gas, and even fresh water.

Divers repairing an undersea cable.

? True or false?

1. Ocean-floor pipes pump oil across the ocean.

2. About four-fifths of the world's goods are transported by sea.

3. We get salt from the ocean by freezing seawater.

See pages 132–133 for the answers

How do we farm fish?

Fish and other marine animals are raised in captivity in the sea for us to eat. This is called fish farming. Salmon and sea bass, along with shellfish, such as oysters, mussels, and shrimp, are often reared. Seaweed can also be grown on fish farms.

Today, more than half of all the seafood eaten in the world comes from fish farms.

Is fish farming bad for the environment?

Chemicals used to keep fish healthy can pollute the water and threaten other sea life. If waste fish-food and poop build up, they can cause harmful blooms of micro-algae.

Seaweed
Strings of seaweed help to improve the quality of the water. The seaweed is also grown for food and used to make other things, such as fertilizer.

Fish farm

In some fish farms, several types of fish and sea animal are raised together. In this farm, the waste from the fish provides nutrients for mussels and sea cucumbers growing nearby.

Mussels

Long chains of mussels grow on ropes that hang from floating buoys. The mussels feed by filtering nutrients from the fish waste out of the water.

Sea bass

Fish such as sea bass, sea bream, and amberjacks are reared in a net near the shore. They are fed specially made pellets to help them grow quickly.

Sea cucumber

Waste from the fish drifts down and is eaten by sea cucumbers below, so the waste does not pollute the water. The sea cucumbers can also be eaten.

? Quick quiz

1. What do sea cucumbers eat in fish farms?

2. What kind of sea animal is a mussel?

3. Where in the ocean are sea bream usually reared?

See pages 132–133 for the answers

What causes a shipwreck?

Many ships that lie wrecked on the seabed were overwhelmed by violent storms. Others met disaster when they struck icebergs, reefs, or rocks, or else were sunk in battle. Some were so poorly built that they should never have set sail!

SS Central America

Laden with passengers and gold, this paddle steamer was caught up in a hurricane off the east coast of the US in 1857. It sank with the loss of 425 lives and all the gold.

MS World Discoverer

In 2000, this cruise ship hit a reef in the South Pacific. Luckily, everyone on board was rescued. The ship can still be seen today, lying on its side in a shallow bay.

Reef

Hurricane

Which is the deepest shipwreck?

In 1944, the American destroyer USS *Johnston* was sunk by Japanese warships off the coast of the Philippines in the Western Pacific. It now lies 20,406 ft (6,220 m) beneath the waves.

? Quick quiz

1. What caused the *Titanic* to sink?

2. What was *Central America* carrying, apart from passengers?

See pages 132–133 for the answers

RMS *Titanic*

In 1912, the luxury liner *Titanic* was on its first ever voyage when it collided with an iceberg and plunged to the bottom of the Atlantic.

Vasa

This Swedish warship was badly designed. It didn't even need a storm, just a mere gust of wind, to blow it over on its first voyage in 1628.

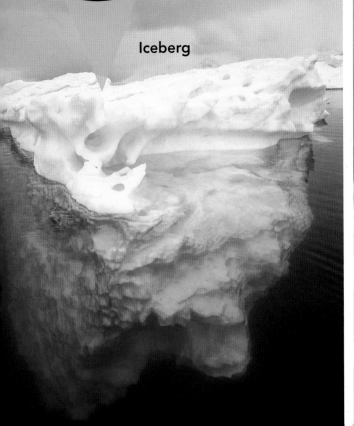

Iceberg

Ocean winds

Then...

This picture shows the Banded Glacier in Washington state in 1960. Glaciers are huge ice "rivers" that flow slowly over the land.

Most of the extra heat produced by global warming is absorbed by the ocean.

Do rising sea levels affect humans?

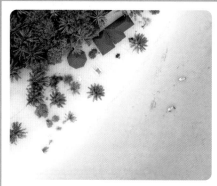

Low-lying islands, such as the Maldives in the Indian Ocean, may disappear under the waves if sea levels keep rising. Many coastal cities throughout the world will be at risk of flooding in the future.

Are sea levels rising?

Yes! Planet Earth's temperatures are rising and causing glaciers and ice sheets to melt. This meltwater gets added to the ocean, making sea levels rise. Ocean water expands (takes up more space) as it warms, which makes sea levels rise even more.

...and now

This is the Banded Glacier in 2016. Global warming has caused it to melt and shrink since 1960. The lake at its bottom has grown much larger.

What is global warming?

Global warming is the gradual increase of the Earth's average temperature due to human activity. When we burn fossil fuels (coal, oil, and gas), we release carbon dioxide and other gases into the atmosphere. These gases trap the sun's heat, making Earth warmer.

The atmosphere naturally traps some heat.

Carbon dioxide and other greenhouse gases build up in the atmosphere.

Sun

Burning fossil fuels produces carbon dioxide.

Heat from the sun enters the atmosphere.

? Quick quiz

1. What does carbon dioxide gas in the atmosphere do?

2. Are Earth's glaciers and ice sheets getting bigger or smaller?

3. What happens to ocean water when it gets warmer?

See pages 132–133 for the answers

Why is plastic so harmful to ocean life?

Plastic poses many dangers to ocean life. Some animals are injured or killed when they get caught up in plastic waste or if they mistake plastic objects for food. Toxic chemicals in plastics may also be poisoning the ocean animals that eat them.

Plastic nets

Animals can get tangled up in old plastic fishing nets dumped at sea. The nets often cause deep cuts when the animals try to wriggle free.

A plastic bag was found at the bottom of the Mariana Trench—the deepest place in the ocean.

Microplastics

Waves and sunlight break plastic into tiny pieces. Small animals that filter food from the water may accidentally eat these "microplastics."

Floating plastic

Due to currents, plastic often collects in areas of the ocean called garbage patches. Other plastic washes up on beaches, causing danger to shore life.

How can plastic end up on your plate?

Plastics can pass along the food chain and end up in the fish on your plate. Small animals that eat microplastics are eaten by bigger animals, which are then preyed on by even larger sea creatures.

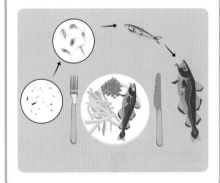

Eating plastic

To a green turtle, a plastic bag resembles a tasty jellyfish. If eaten, an object like this can choke an animal or block its stomach.

? Quick quiz

1. What are microplastics?

2. What can a floating plastic bag look like to a turtle?

3. Where does most of the plastic in the sea end up?

See pages 132–133 for the answers

Sunken plastic

Most of the plastic in the ocean eventually sinks to the bottom. It remains a menace to seafloor animals for many years.

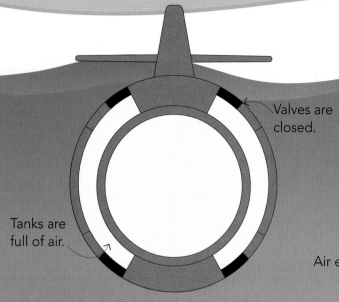

Valves are closed.

Tanks are full of air.

Diving

To dive, the valves open and seawater floods the tanks. The submarine is now heavier than the water, so it sinks. The more water it takes in, the deeper it sinks.

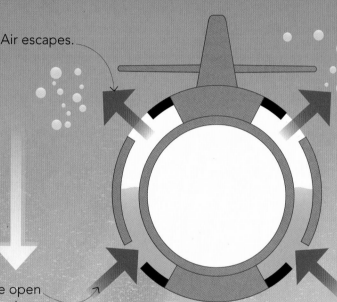

Air escapes.

Floating

When the submarine's tanks are full of air, it floats at the ocean's surface. The air is less dense than the water, so it keeps the heavy submarine afloat.

Valves are open and the tanks fill with water.

How does a submarine dive?

A submarine dives by changing its buoyancy. It makes itself denser (heavier) or less dense (lighter) than the water around it. It has tanks that it fills with water to dive, and then pumps full of air to surface.

? Quick quiz

1. What does a submarine fill its tanks with to dive?

2. What does a submarine use to turn left or right?

3. If a submarine is made less dense (lighter) than water, does it rise or sink?

See pages 132–133 for the answers

Air is pumped into the tanks.

Valves close.

Water is forced out.

Rising

To rise, the valves close and the tanks are filled with air from a separate compartment. The air forces the water out of the tanks. The submarine is now lighter, so it rises in the water.

What is a submersible?

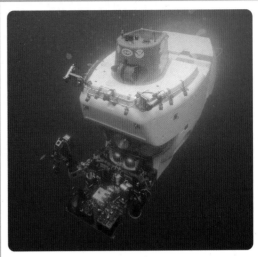

Submersibles are small submarines that carry just a few people. A submersible usually stays linked to a ship on the surface, which supplies it with power and air. Others can move freely on their own.

How do submarines steer?

At the back of a submarine are two upright rudders that swivel to turn the submarine left or right. There are also pairs of horizontal "wings" at the front and rear, called bow and stern planes. These swivel to tilt the submarine up or down when rising or diving.

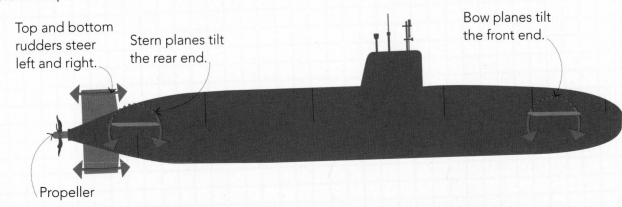

Top and bottom rudders steer left and right.

Stern planes tilt the rear end.

Bow planes tilt the front end.

Propeller

Ocellated brain coral

This stony, or hard, coral is at risk from coral bleaching caused by the warming of the ocean due to climate change.

Vulnerable

A little porpoise called the vaquita is the world's rarest sea mammal—there are fewer than 20 adults left.

Humphead wrasse

This huge fish is a luxury food in some parts of the world. It is endangered by overfishing and the destruction of its coral reef habitat by coral bleaching.

Endangered

Which sea creatures are in danger?

Many ocean animals are under threat due to human activities. Scientists put animals in categories depending on how endangered they are. The most at-risk animals are "critically endangered." If we do not help these animals, they will soon become extinct.

Critically Endangered

Hawksbill turtle

Hawksbills are caught for their shells, which are made into jewelry and ornaments. Building along coasts has destroyed many of their nesting beaches.

Sperm whale

Huge numbers of sperm whales were once killed for the wax and oil in their bodies. Now that whaling is banned, their numbers are slowly recovering.

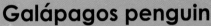

Endangered

Galápagos penguin

This penguin lives on the Galápagos Islands in the Pacific. It is threatened by pollution and bycatch and by the introduction of disease-carrying animals, such as rats, to the islands.

Critically Endangered

Common skate

This slow-growing fish takes about 11 years to reach breeding age. It cannot breed quickly enough to replace fish lost to overfishing and bycatch.

? Quick quiz

1. Why are hawksbill turtles caught?

2. Which type of animal is most at risk—"vulnerable" or "critically endangered"?

3. What does "extinct" mean?

See pages 132–133 for the answers

What happened to Steller's sea cow?

A relative of manatees and dugongs, Steller's sea cow lived in the chilly Bering Sea in the North Pacific around the 1700s. In just 30 years, this slow-moving, easily caught mammal was hunted to extinction by Europeans for its meat, fat, and skin.

How do hurricanes form?

Also called typhoons and cyclones, hurricanes form when the sun's heat stirs up warm, moist air over the sea in tropical regions. Hurricanes can bring howling winds that flatten buildings, torrential rain that causes flooding, and huge waves that swamp the coast.

The largest hurricane ever was 1,380 miles (2,220 km) across—about half the width of the US!

1. Clouds form

The sun's heat causes surface water from the ocean to evaporate. Rising water vapor condenses when it meets cold air, forming storm clouds.

Earth's rotation makes the clouds spin.

The sea must reach at least 80°F (27°C) before hurricanes can form.

2. Winds blow.

A column of warm, moist air spirals upward, spreading out at the top to form a huge wheel of cloud. Swirling winds blow around the column.

Are there tornadoes at sea?

Tornadoes are like hurricanes, but are smaller, briefer, and more unpredictable. While most tornadoes occur on land, there are tornadoes at sea—these are called waterspouts. They form when rising air below a storm starts to spin. A waterspout can suck up water from the sea and can capsize or wreck boats. However, tornadoes at sea are less violent than on land.

What is a storm surge?

A sudden rise in sea levels caused by a storm is called a storm surge. It happens when winds push water into a peak that crashes onto the shore. Storm surges can flood coastal areas, especially when they happen at high tide.

3. Hurricane!

As the pressure falls in the column at the storm's center, called the eye, the winds around it blow more strongly. The air inside the eye is calm.

? Quick quiz

1. Where do hurricanes form?
   a) polar regions
   b) temperate regions
   c) tropical regions

2. What is a tornado at sea called?
   a) a waterspout
   b) a geyser
   c) a maelstrom

See pages 132–133 for the answers

When is fishing a problem?

Fishing is a problem when we catch too many fish. As fewer fish breed, so fewer young are born, and fish numbers dwindle. Some types of fishing also accidentally catch a lot of fish and other sea animals that aren't wanted. This is called bycatch.

Some scientists say that most of the world's fish stock could be wiped out by 2050.

Bottom trawling

To catch deep-sea fish, a net is dragged along the bottom and the net may plow up the seabed. There is often bycatch, because everything in the way of the net gets swept up, too.

Gillnets

Fish swim headfirst into this hanging net and get caught by the gills as they try to wriggle back out. Turtles and mammals such as dolphins may get trapped and drown.

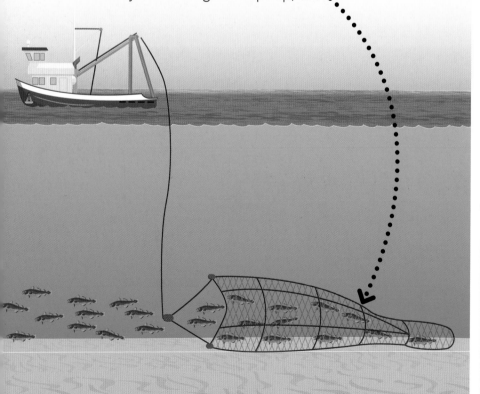

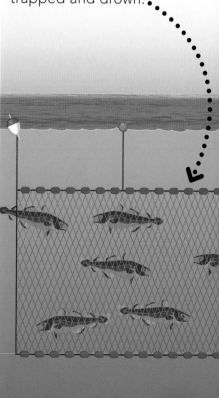

What is whaling?

We used to catch lots of whales for their meat, oil, skin, and bones. This practice, called whaling, led to some species nearly becoming extinct. Today, most countries have banned whaling.

**2¼ lb (1 kg)
shrimp**

**13 lb (6 kg)
other fish**

Is shrimping a problem?

Shrimp are nutritious, but for every 2¼ lb (1 kg) of shrimp caught there can be 13 lb (6 kg) or more of bycatch. About one-third of all the world's bycatch is from shrimping.

Purse seine

A school of fish is encircled by a wall of netting. The bottom of the net is then closed, and the net is hauled in. There is usually less bycatch than with some other types of fishing.

? Quick quiz

1. What is bycatch?

2. Is whaling banned in every country?

See pages 132–133 for the answers

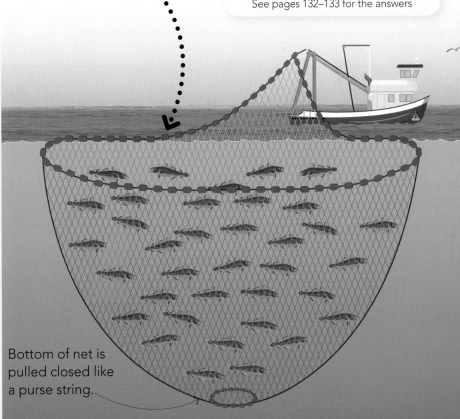

Bottom of net is pulled closed like a purse string.

Step 1

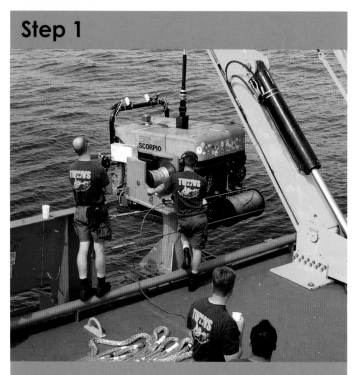

Launching

This underwater robot is an ROV. It is being taken to the dive site by ship and lowered into the water. Cables supply the ROV with power and send data between the robot and the ship.

ROVs with cameras are used in search-and-rescue missions in murky water and under ice.

Step 2

Traveling

The ROV works like a remote-controlled submarine. Operators on the ship steer the ROV to its destination by sending instructions to the robot through the cables.

How do underwater robots work?

Underwater robots investigate the ocean—searching for wrecks, checking out seafloor pipelines, and studying marine life. They have no crew and are cheaper to build and operate than submarines. There are two types: remotely operated vehicles (ROVs) and autonomous underwater vehicles (AUVs).

How do AUVs work?

An AUV is an underwater robot that can work on its own once it is launched. It is not connected to a ship on the surface. It follows instructions programmed into its onboard computer.

? Quick quiz

1. Which type of underwater robot is connected to a surface ship by cables, an AUV or an ROV?

2. What controls an AUV?

3. How does an ROV get to the dive site?

See pages 132–133 for the answers

Step 3

Controlling

On board the ship, the operators watch video footage from the ROV's cameras and study the information the robot sends back to the ship. They decide what the ROV does next.

Step 4

Collecting

The ROV may have sensors that collect data about the water's temperature, pressure, and saltiness. It may also have mechanical arms that the operators use to collect samples.

Exploring

Small craft investigate places in the deep sea where divers cannot go to. They examine ocean conditions and discover new species.

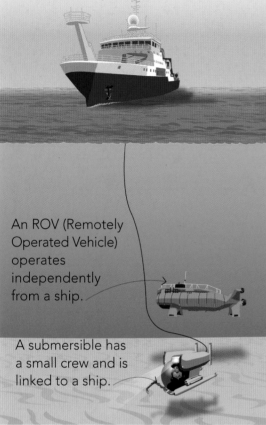

An ROV (Remotely Operated Vehicle) operates independently from a ship.

A submersible has a small crew and is linked to a ship.

Mapping

Sonar ships bounce sounds off the seabed. The echoes that come back help scientists build up a picture of the seafloor.

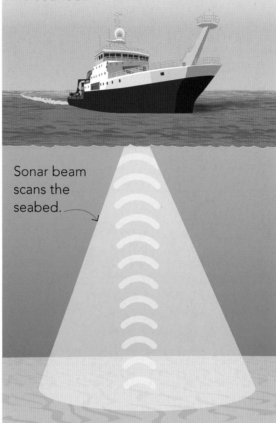

Sonar beam scans the seabed.

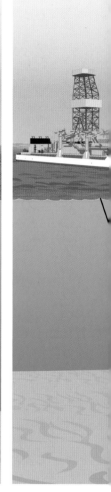

How do we study the oceans?

To find out more about the oceans we use divers, ships, underwater craft, satellites, and observatories. Scientists called oceanographers study ocean water, rocks, the weather above the ocean, and the life within it.

In 1957, US geologists Marie Tharp and Bruce Heezen made the first seafloor map of the world's oceans.

Drilling

Long drills collect samples of sediment and rock. The samples tell researchers about the makeup of the ocean floor.

Drills can go several miles into seabed rock.

Observing

An ocean observatory is a set of instruments fixed to the seabed. It can keep a check of many things, including the temperature and saltiness of the water, and the amount of carbon dioxide in it.

The observatory sends data to a buoy on the surface.

Satellite study

Satellites collect information about the ocean. They receive data from buoys—devices that float in the ocean. Satellites help us measure ocean temperatures and sea levels. They also are used to map the seafloor, forecast hurricanes, track migrating animals, and more.

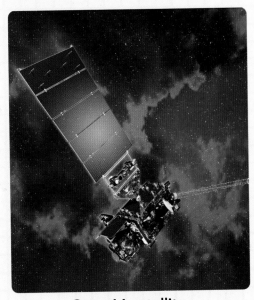

Goes-16 satellite

What do marine biologists do?

Marine biologists study how animals, plants, algae, and tiny organisms called microbes live together in the ocean, and how human activity affects them. They work in laboratories and on ships. They also dive to take samples and explore in submersibles.

? Quick quiz

1. What do research ships use to map the seafloor?
   a) telescopes
   b) sonar
   c) a ruler

2. What do marine biologists do?
   a) map the seafloor
   b) study ocean life
   c) drill for oil on the seabed

See pages 132–133 for the answers

How can we take care of the oceans?

Ocean life faces many challenges and threats, such as global warming, pollution, and overfishing. These are huge and complex problems, but there is much that we can do to care for the oceans and protect the life they contain.

Use clean energy

Switching from fossil fuels to wind, solar, and hydroelectric power (using water to generate electricity) helps our planet. These energy sources don't produce global-warming gases.

Protect animals

Setting up areas of the ocean as marine parks where fishing and hunting are either banned or controlled helps to protect marine animals. Park rangers can help animals live and breed in safety.

Save habitats

Planting new seedlings can restore damaged mangrove forests and seagrass meadows. Passing laws to limit building along coasts can protect habitats from damage in the future.

Should we stop eating seafood?

Seafood is healthy and tasty. However, we should make sure that any seafood we eat is caught or farmed in a way that doesn't harm other animals or marine habitats. One way to do this is to look for labels on seafood that say "responsibly sourced" or "sustainably sourced."

? *True or false?*

1. Hydroelectric power uses wind to generate electricity.

2. Animals are protected in areas of the ocean called marine parks.

3. Fossil fuels are good for the environment.

See pages 132–133 for the answers

Fish responsibly

We can fish in ways that don't harm the seabed and that catch as few unwanted animals as possible. If we take fewer fish from the sea, fish populations will be able to grow.

Clean beaches

Keeping beaches clean prevents animals from being injured by trash. If we use less plastic and recycle the plastic we do use, we can help to stop plastic from getting into the sea.

Reduce pollution

Waste water often contains harmful chemicals that find their way into the ocean. At home, we can choose nontoxic detergents and cleaning products that are not harmful to wildlife.

Answers

Page 9 1) Hot volcanic gases and water vapor. 2) Gravity stops the oceans from flying off into space.

Page 11 1) False. It was a type of reptile. 2) False. It was the Panthalassic Ocean. 3) True.

Page 13 1) Oceans are larger than seas. 2) Five. 3) Yes.

Page 14 The sunlit zone.

Page 17 1) The Indian Ocean. 2) The Great Barrier Reef. 3) Fish. Seabirds and whales feed on the fish.

Page 19 1) False. Blue light travels deepest. 2) True. 3) False. Algae turn seawater green.

Page 21 1) True. Currents are driven by the wind and Earth's rotation. 2) False. The Gulf Stream brings warmer water to northern Europe. 3) True.

Page 23 1) b. 2) c.

Page 25 1) False. It turns from liquid to gas. 2) False. A long time in the future, Earth will be a dry planet. 3) True.

Page 27 1) False. Salt is sodium chloride. 2) True. 3) False—97 percent of Earth's water is salty.

Page 29 Breakers.

Page 31 1) Generally every six hours. 2) The moon's gravity. 3) Two.

Page 35 1) False. They are usually caused by earthquakes at sea, and sometimes by underwater landslides and volcanic eruptions. 2) False. "Tsunami" means "harbor wave." 3) False. Tsunamis get bigger as the water gets shallower.

Page 37 b.

Page 39 1) Around the edges of the Pacific Ocean. 2) It cools and forms a black, glassy skin. 3) Magma builds up and burns through the crust.

Page 41 1) True. 2) False. Fresh water is less dense than seawater. 3) False. The molecules in ice are farther apart than those in liquid water.

Page 42 1) True. 2) False. Few undersea volcanoes reach the surface and form islands. 3) True.

Page 45 1) Rocks worn by waves into smooth, rounded shapes. 2) In sheltered places, such as estuaries and bays. 3) When softer rock between two bits of harder rock gets eroded away, it creates a bay.

Page 47 1) Algae. 2) The tide carries foam onto the shore. 3) A whitish color.

Page 49 1) They collide, and one plate gets pushed under another. 2) Iceland.

Page 51 1) a. 2) a.

Page 55 1) Warm, shallow coastal waters. 2) Because they graze on seagrass. 3) It gets buried and safely trapped in the seabed.

Page 56 1) True. 2) False. Sea pens do live on the seabed, but they are not fish. 3) True.

Page 59 1) b.

Page 61 1) b. 2) b.

Page 63 1) To hunt fish. 2) Brackish water. 3) They are partly or completely covered by water.

Page 64 1) An atoll. 2) Hard coral. 3) Tiny algae.

Page 67 1) Magma. 2) No. It is fueled by jets of hot, mineral-rich water. 3) Dissolved minerals.

Page 69 1) In tropical regions. 2) Saltwater crocodile. 3) It absorbs oxygen through its moist skin.

Page 71 1) It has "antifreeze" chemicals in its blood. 2) A mammal. 3) Up to 20 in (50 cm) thick.

Page 73 1) b. 2) a.

Page 75 1) No. It is a seaweed, a type of algae. 2) To feed on plankton. 3) Holdfasts.

Page 79 1) No animals prey on orcas in the wild. 2) Yes. 3) A food chain.

Page 81 1) Because the water no longer supports their bodies. 2) An invertebrate. 3) No.

Page 83 1) False. They decorate their bodies with objects that they find on the seabed. 2) True. 3) False. Stonefish are very fasteaters—sucking in prey in less than a second!

Page 85 1) True. 2) False. An octopus has nine brains—one central brain in its head and eight other brains, one in each arm. 3) False. It collects empty clam shells.

Page 86 1) False. Bacteria in their bodies use chemicals to make light. 2) False. Red light does not reach the deep ocean. 3) True.

Page 89 1) Sperm whale. 2) 300. 3) A pod.

Page 91 1) c. 2) b.

Page 92 1) It flaps fins on its head. 2) A sea cucumber. 3) With its chin barbels.

Page 95 1) a. 2) c.

Page 97 A penguin—an Antarctic emperor penguin.

Page 99 1) Yes. 2) The sand lance. 3) To keep parasites away from its skin.

Page 101 It is coating its feathers with oil. This is called preening.

Page 103 1) A zombie worm. 2) No. Many are eaten before they reach the seafloor. 3) The hard parts.

Page 104 1) Yes—there are sea snakes, but not giant ones. 2) A giant squid. 3) No. Giant oarfish are gentle plankton feeders.

Page 109 1) True. 2) True. 3) False. We get salt from the ocean by evaporating seawater.

Page 111 1) Waste from the fish being farmed. 2) A shellfish. 3) Near the shore.

Page 113 1) It collided with an iceberg. 2) Gold.

Page 115 1) It traps heat. 2) Smaller. 3) It expands.

Page 117 1) Tiny pieces of plastic. 2) A jellyfish. 3) On the bottom of the ocean.

Page 118 1) Water. 2) Rudders. 3) It rises.

Page 121 1) For their shells. 2) Critically endangered. 3) Died out completely.

Page 123 1) c. 2) a.

Page 125 1) Bycatch is accidentally caught fish and other sea animals that aren't wanted. 2) Whaling is banned in most countries, but not all.

Page 127 1) An ROV. 2) An onboard computer. 3) It is taken there by ship.

Page 129 1) b. 2) b.

Page 131 1) False. Hydroelectric power uses water to generate electricity. 2) True. 3) False. Fossil fuels are bad for the environment because they produce global warming gases.

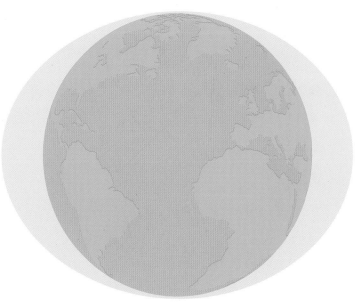

Quiz your friends!

Who knows the most about the oceans? Test your friends and family with these tricky questions. See pages 136–137 for the answers.

Questions

1. How long did the "snowball Earth" ice age last?

6. WHAT FELL OFF A **SHIP IN 1992** AND REVEALED A LOT **ABOUT OCEAN CURRENTS**?

9. This is the **top of the tallest ocean mountain**—what is it called?

3. Can you **name Earth's five oceans**?

2. Which animal makes wiggly piles of mud like this?

4. Why is this **hairy crab** called a **yeti crab**?

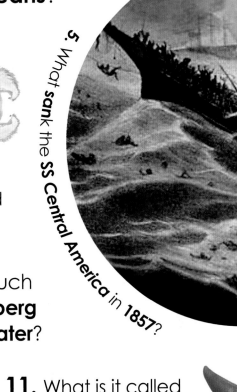

5. What **sank** the **SS Central America** in **1857**?

8. How much of an **iceberg** is **underwater**?

7. Which **animals prey** on leopard seals?

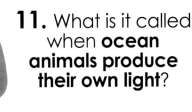

11. What is it called when **ocean animals produce their own light**?

12. Why are **sea levels rising**?

10. What are hot, **mineral-rich jets** of water on the **deep-ocean floor** called?

13. What are the **rocky slabs that make up Earth's outer layer**, or crust, called?

14. A **blue whale weighs** the **same** as how many **African elephants**?

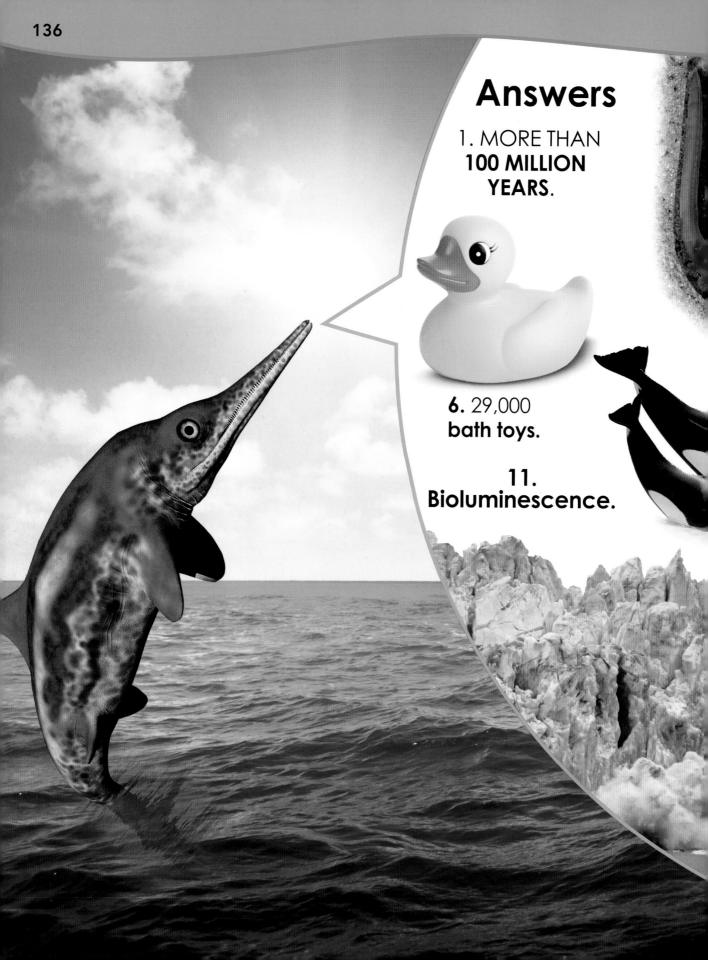

Answers

1. MORE THAN **100 MILLION YEARS**.

6. 29,000 **bath toys.**

11. Bioluminescence.

2. A lugworm.

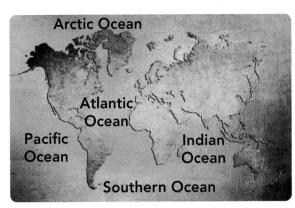

Arctic Ocean

Atlantic Ocean

Pacific Ocean

Indian Ocean

Southern Ocean

3. Atlantic Ocean, Pacific Ocean, Indian Ocean, Southern Ocean, Arctic Ocean.

4. It is named after the yeti—the legendary "abominable snowman" said to live in the Himalayas.

5. A hurricane.

7. Orcas

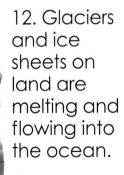

8. About 90 percent!

9. MAUNA KEA, IN HAWAII.

10. HYDROTHERMAL VENTS.

12. Glaciers and ice sheets on land are melting and flowing into the ocean.

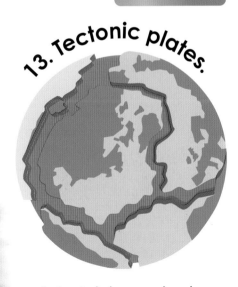

13. Tectonic plates.

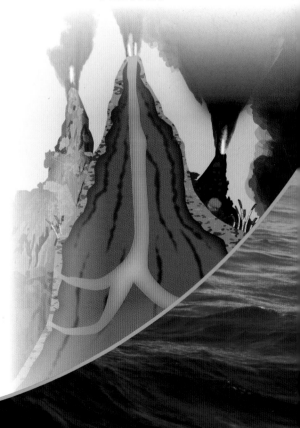

14. A blue whale weighs the same as **30 African elephants**.

Glossary

abyss
Cold, dark layer of the ocean between the midnight and hadal zones

abyssal plain
Huge, flat area of the deep-ocean floor

algae
Simple, plantlike living things that make their own food using energy from sunlight

bioluminescence
Light produced by living things

blowhole
Hole in the head of a dolphin or whale that is used to breathe air at the surface

blubber
Fatty layer under the skin of sea mammals that traps body heat

brackish
Water that is salty, but not as salty as seawater

bycatch
Unwanted fish and seafood that are caught accidentally

cephalopod
Mollusk with a large head and tentacles, such as a squid or octopus

continental shelf
Relatively flat and shallow seafloor that surrounds a continent

crustacean
Invertebrate with a skeleton on the outside of its body; crabs and lobsters are crustaceans

current
Large, regular flow of ocean water

dorsal fin
Fin on the back of a fish or marine mammal

estuary
River mouth, where water empties into the sea

evaporate
To change from a liquid into a gas

extinct
Died out completely

fossil fuel
Fuel made from the buried remains of long-dead organisms; coal, oil, and gas are fossil fuels

gills
Organs that absorb oxygen from water, used for breathing by fish and some other marine animals

glacier
Slow-moving river of freshwater ice on land

groundwater
Water underground

gyre
Large area in the ocean with rotating currents

hadal zone
Ocean's deepest zone, in deep trenches, where it is icy cold, dark, and water pressure is huge

hydroelectric power
Electricity produced by harnessing the energy of flowing water

hydrothermal vent
Opening on the deep-ocean floor where hot, mineral-rich water gushes out from Earth's interior

ice age
Long period of very cold conditions on Earth, when much of the planet was covered with ice

ice sheet
Huge, permanent sheet of freshwater ice on land

iceberg
Big floating lump of freshwater ice in the ocean; icebergs break off ice sheets and glaciers

invertebrate
Animal without a backbone

mammal
Animal with hair that feeds its young on milk

mangrove
Tree (or forest of trees) that grows in salty water in coastal regions

marine biologist
Scientist who studies life in the ocean

marine park
Protected area of the ocean that is set aside so that marine life can live undisturbed by humans

marine snow
Nonstop fall of tiny bits of dead organisms through the ocean down to the seafloor

meltwater
Water from melted glaciers and ice sheets

microbes
Microscopic living things, such as bacteria

microplastics
Tiny pieces of plastic that form when sunlight and waves break up plastic objects in the ocean

mid-ocean ridge
Underwater mountain range that forms where two tectonic plates pull apart on the ocean floor

midnight zone
Area of the ocean below the twilight zone, where no light reaches

mollusk
Soft-bodied invertebrate, often with a hard shell; clams, mussels, and limpets are mollusks

mudflat
Large, flat area of sand and mud near the shore that is uncovered at low tide

ocean trench
Deep canyon in the ocean floor that forms where one tectonic plate is pushed beneath another

oceanic crust
Earth's crust under the deep oceans

oceanic island
Island that forms when an undersea volcano rises above the ocean's surface

oceanographer
Scientist who studies the ocean

ooze
Layer of soft mud on the ocean floor formed from the rotting remains of dead organisms

overfishing
Taking so many fish or other marine creatures from the sea that their numbers fall drastically

pectoral fin
Fin found in fish and other sea animals

phytoplankton
Tiny ocean algae that drift with the current

polyp
Small animal with a cup-shaped body and a mouth surrounded by tentacles that lives fixed to the seabed; corals are polyps

saltmarsh
Grassland on the coast that gets flooded by the ocean at high tide

sea ice
Frozen seawater

seamount
Lone mountain on the seafloor

sediment
Layer of sand, mud, and other material that settles on the ocean floor

sonar
Using echoes from sound waves to build up "sound pictures" for navigating or making maps of the seafloor

spawn
To reproduce by releasing eggs and sperm into water

spore
Single cell that can grow into a new living thing; algae, fungi, and some plants use spores to reproduce

storm surge
Unusually high rise in sea levels caused by a storm

submersible
Small underwater vehicle that can carry just a few people

sunlit zone
Uppermost layer of the ocean

swim bladder
Gas-filled bag inside a fish that allows the fish to control the level at which it floats

tide
Daily rise or fall of the ocean caused by the pull of the moon's gravity

tropics
Warm regions found around the equator

twilight zone
Part of the ocean below the sunlight zone where light begins to fade out

upthrust
Force that pushes upward against objects in water

valve
Faucetlike device that controls the flow of a liquid or gas

water cycle
Nonstop movement of water between the ocean, atmosphere, and land

water vapor
Water in the form of a gas

waterspout
Tornado at sea

whirlpool
Swirling mass of water in the sea, into which objects may be pulled

zooplankton
Tiny sea creatures that drift with the current

zooxanthellae
Microscopic algae

Index

Acknowledgments

DORLING KINDERSLEY would like to thank: Katie Lawrence for editorial support; Caroline Hunt for proofreading; Helen Peters for the index.

Consultant Dr Dave Pawson, Senior Scientist, Emeritus, Curator of Echinoderms National Museum of Natural History, Smithsonian

Smithsonian Enterprises

Kealy Gordon Product Development Manager

Jill Corcoran Director, Licensed Publishing

Brigid Ferraro Vice President, Business Development and Licensing

Carol LeBlanc President

The publisher would like to thank the following for their kind permission to reproduce their photographs:

(Key: a-above; b-below/bottom; c-center; f-far; l-left; r-right; t-top)

2 naturepl.com: Chris & Monique Fallows (crb). 4 Dreamstime.com: Joan Carles Juarez (crb). 5 Alamy Stock Photo: David Chapman (tc); Helmut Corneli (c). Dreamstime.com: Vladimir Seliverstov (bc). 6 Science Photo Library: Dr Ken Macdonald. 9 Dreamstime.com: Aoleshko (ca); NASA: MSFC / Aaron Kingery (tc). 10 Alamy Stock Photo: Hypersphere / Science Photo Library (bl); MasPix (bc). 10–11 Dreamstime.com: Surasak Suwanmake (Background). 12 Dreamstime.com: Antartis (bl). 12–13 123RF.com: Iakov Kalinin (t). Dreamstime.com: Ethan Daniels (bc). 13 Alamy Stock Photo: ManuelMata (br). Dreamstime.com: Goldghost (cla). 14 Alamy Stock Photo: NOAA (cr); Oceans Image / Avalon.red (ca, crb). Fotolia: Karl Bolf (cra). 15 Alamy Stock Photo: Pally (cra); Norbert Wu / Minden Pictures (c). Science Photo Library: Claus Lunau (cla). 16 Dreamstime.com: Martinmark (cl); Vlad1949 (bc). 17 Dreamstime.com: Steve Boice (tc). Getty Images / iStock: ShaneMyersPhoto (cr). 18 Dreamstime.com: Giovanni Gagliardi (clb). 19 Dreamstime.com: Andreykuzmin (cra). 21 Dreamstime.com: Tirrasa (bl). 22 Alamy Stock Photo: Konrad Wothe / Minden Pictures (cl); Norbert Wu / Minden Pictures (cb). Dreamstime.com: Luyag2. 23 Alamy Stock Photo: Jessica Wilson / NASA / Science History Images (ca). 24 Alamy Stock Photo: Mark Garlick / Science Photo Library (bl). 26 Alamy Stock Photo: Tracey Whitefoot (tr). Science Photo Library: Dr Ken Macdonald (br). 27 123RF.com: Irina Belousa (crb). Dreamstime.com: Kanawat (bl); Dmitry Naumov (tl). 29 Dreamstime.com: Epicstock (cra); Julien Jean (cla). 31 Alamy Stock Photo: Adam Silver (cb); Tom Uhlman (cr). 32 Alamy Stock Photo: Galaxiid (t); Doug Perrine (b). 33 Dreamstime.com: Amilevin (t). 34 Alamy Stock Photo: Granger Historical Picture Archive NYC (bl). 34–35 Dreamstime.com: Photomo. 37 NASA: (tr). 38 Getty Images: Science Photo Library / Mark Garlick (clb). 38–39 Alamy Stock Photo: Doug Perrine. 40 Alamy Stock Photo: Insignis Photography (cl). 40–41 Dreamstime.com: Marc-andré Le Tourneux. 42 Alamy Stock Photo: Galaxiid (cl). 44 Dreamstime.com: Amilevin (cra); Viktor Gladkov. 45 Dreamstime.com: Jon Bilous. 46–47 Dreamstime.com: Dasya11. 47 Getty Images: The Asahi Shimbun (br). Science Photo Library: Dennis Kunkel Microscopy (tc). 48–49 naturepl.com: Wild Wonders of Europe / Lundgre. 50 Alamy Stock Photo: Helmut Corneli (bl); FLPA (c). 50–51 Alamy Stock Photo: ArteSub (t). 52 Alamy Stock Photo: Artur Golbert (b); Nature Picture Library / Alex Mustard (r). 54 Alamy Stock Photo: Nature Picture Library / Alex Mustard (bl). Dreamstime.com: Idreamphotos (clb). Getty Images / iStock: lemga (cl). 54–55 Getty Images / iStock: E+ / lindsay_imagery. 55 Alamy Stock Photo: Biosphoto (tr). Dreamstime.com: Jonmilnes (tc); Alexander Ogurtsov (tl). Getty Images / iStock: RibeirodosSantos (tr). 57 Alamy Stock Photo: Nature Picture Library / Constantinos Petrinos (tr); VWPics / Kelvin Aitken (clb); Nature Picture Library (crb). Depositphotos Inc: YAYImages (cb). Dreamstime.com: Emilio100 (tc); Suwat Sirivutcharungchit (tl). 59 Alamy Stock Photo: David Chapman (tl); B. Mete Uz (tr). 60–61 Dreamstime.com: Animaflora. 60 Dreamstime.com: Nigel Hoy (br). Science Photo Library: Dennis Kunkel Microscopy (clb). 61 Dreamstime.com: Michael Mill (bl). 62–63 Dreamstime.com: Mihai Andritoiu. 63 Dreamstime.com: Harry Collins (bc); Brian Kushner (bl). 64 Alamy Stock Photo: Stocktrek Images, Inc. / Ethan Daniels (cl). Dreamstime.com: Fabio Lamanna (bl); Debra Law (clb). 64–65 Alamy Stock Photo: WaterFrame_dpr. 65 Alamy Stock Photo: blickwinkel / McPHOTO / BIO (br). 66 Alamy Stock Photo: Adisha Pramod (tr). Science Photo Library: NOAA Okeanos Explorer Program, Galapagos Rift Expedition 2011 (cl). 67 Alamy Stock Photo: Don Johnston_PL (cra). 68 Dreamstime.com: Cowboy54 (clb); Feathercollector (cl). Getty Images / iStock: miralex (bl). 68–69 Alamy Stock Photo: Reinhard Dirscherl. 69 Alamy Stock Photo: Adrian Hepworth (tr). Dreamstime.com: Ecophoto (bc). 70 Dreamstime.com: Vladimir Seliverstov (bl). naturepl.com: Jordi Chias (br). 70–71 Pixabay: (tc). 71 Dreamstime.com: Musat Christian (bl); Ondřej Prosický (cla). 72 Alamy Stock Photo: Artur Golbert (cb); Andrey Nekrasov (tr). Dreamstime.com: John Anderson (bl); Anthony Aneese Totah Jr (crb); Seadam (clb). 72–73 naturepl.com: Shane Gross (bc). 73 Alamy Stock Photo: imageBROKER / Norbert Probst (tl). Dreamstime.com: Isselee (cl); Daniel Poloha (tc); Joan Carles Juarez (bc). 74 Alamy Stock Photo: Barbara Ash (cra). Depositphotos Inc: kostadive (cr). Getty Images / iStock: KGrif (cl). naturepl.com: Ralph Pace (cra). Shutterstock.com: Ethan Daniels (br). 75 Dreamstime.com: Kelpfish (cll). naturepl.com: DOC WHITE (cr). 76 Alamy Stock Photo: Gerry McLaughlin (b). Shutterstock.com: FanyArt (t).

77 Getty Images / iStock: Nigel Marsh. 78 Alamy Stock Photo: Paul Fleet (c). Dreamstime.com: Derek Rogers (clb). 79 Alamy Stock Photo: Nature Picture Library / David Tipling (c). Dreamstime.com: John Anderson (cr); Natallia Yatskova (ca); Mark Aplet (cra). Science Photo Library: Wim Van Egmond (tc). 80–81 Alamy Stock Photo: Helmut Corneli. 82 Dreamstime.com: Ethan Daniels (tr); Irko Van Der Heide (tl). 83 Alamy Stock Photo: imageBROKER / SeaTops (bc). Dreamstime.com: Jxpfeer (tr). Shutterstock.com: Kris Wiktor (tl). 84–85 Alamy Stock Photo: Biosphoto. 85 Dreamstime.com: Gary Webber (br). 86 Alamy Stock Photo: Minden Pictures / Norbert Wu (bl); Nature Picture Library / David Shale (clb). 86–87 Alamy Stock Photo: Pally. 87 Alamy Stock Photo: Bluegreen Pictures / David Shale (bc). 88 Depositphotos Inc: mic1805 (b). 88–89 Dreamstime.com: Slowmotiongli (bc). 89 Alamy Stock Photo: RooM the Agency / ronnisantoso (ca). Dreamstime.com: Pics516 (cla). Getty Images / iStock: vladoskan (b). 90 Alamy Stock Photo: Poelzer Wolfgang (b). Dreamstime.com: Rkpimages (cb). 91 Alamy Stock Photo: Minden Pictures / Buiten-beeld / Wil Meinderts (tl); Michael Patrick O'Neill (br). 92 Alamy Stock Photo: Norbert Wu / Minden Pictures (c). naturepl.com: David Shale (tc). NOAA: Office of Ocean Exploration and Research, Windows to the Deep 2019 (bl). Science Photo Library: British Antarctic Survey (cla). 93 Alamy Stock Photo: Jane Gould (cr); Minden Pictures / Norbert Wu (cla). NOAA: (tc). 94 Alamy Stock Photo: Biosphoto / Steven Kovacs (cra); WaterFrame_mus (clb). Getty Images / iStock: LUNAMARINA (br). 94–95 Dreamstime.com: Andreykuzmin (b). naturepl.com: Franco Banfi (cb). 95 Alamy Stock Photo: Nature Picture Library (bl). naturepl.com: Chris & Monique Fallows (tl). 96 Alamy Stock Photo: blickwinkel / AGAMI / L. Steijn (bl). 96–97 Dreamstime.com: Ig0rzh. 97 Alamy Stock Photo: Steve Bloom Images / Pal Hermansen (tl). Dreamstime.com: Sergey Uryadnikov (tc). 98 Alamy Stock Photo: David Fleetham. 99 Alamy Stock Photo: Richard Eaker (tr); Pally (tl). Dreamstime.com: Izanbar (bl). Getty Images / iStock: Nigel Marsh (tc). 100–101 Alamy Stock Photo: David Chapman. 101 Alamy Stock Photo: Gerry McLaughlin (br). 102 Henk-Jan Hoving: (cra). 103 Dreamstime.com: Emoke Kupai (cla). 104 Alamy Stock Photo: MichaelGrantWildlife (crb); Pally (clb). Shutterstock.com: FanyArt (cb). 105 Alamy Stock Photo: North Wind Picture Archives (bc). 106 Alamy Stock Photo: Pally (t). 106–107 Alamy Stock Photo: Anthony Pierce (bc). Getty Images / iStock: Androsov (tl). 108 Alamy Stock Photo: Georg Berg (tr); dpa picture alliance (tl). Dreamstime.com: Jane1e (tc). 109 Alamy Stock Photo: AB Forces News Collection (bc). Dreamstime.com: Svetlana Day (tl); Denis Moskvinov (tc); Mr.siwabud Veerapaisarn (cr). 110 Alamy Stock Photo: Pally (bl). Dreamstime.com: Daisuke Kurashima (cra). 111 Dreamstime.com: Cohhuk (c); Ericsch (cb). 112 Alamy Stock Photo: FLHC 3 (cr); Nature Picture Library / Michael Pitts (cl). Getty Images / iStock: Michael Zeigler (bl). NASA: LANCE / EOSDIS Rapid Response (br). 113 Alamy Stock Photo: AA Film Archive (cl). Dreamstime.com: Michalakis Ppalis (br); Alexander Tolstykh (c). naturepl.com: Jeff Vanuga (bl). Courtesy of U.S. Navy: (cla). 114 Depositphotos Inc: Pakhnyushchyy (cra). U.S. Geological Survey. 115 Courtesy of National Park Service, Lewis and Clark National Historic Trail. 116 Alamy Stock Photo: Nature Picture Library / Enrique Lopez-Tapia (cra). Shutterstock.com: IgnacioFPV (b). 116–117 Alamy Stock Photo: Pally (tc). 117 Alamy Stock Photo: Pally (cla). Shutterstock.com: Andriy Nekrasov (bl). 118–119 Dreamstime.com: Dmytro Tolokonov. 119 Woods Hole Oceanographic Institition: (tr). 120 Depositphotos Inc: Vojce (t). Dreamstime.com: Andrey Armyagov (crb); Flyingrussian (cra). 121 Alamy Stock Photo: Avalon.red / Oceans Image (cl); Pally (clb); Universal Images Group North America LLC / Encyclopaedia Britannica Inc. (bc). Depositphotos Inc: mic1805 (b). 123 Getty Images / iStock: koto_feja (ca); Moorefam (cr). 125 Alamy Stock Photo: Historic Images (cla). 126 Alamy Stock Photo: PJF Military Collection (tl). Getty Images: Alexis Rosenfeld (cra). 127 Alamy Stock Photo: Suzanne Long (tc); Simon Price (cl). NOAA: (crb). 129 Getty Images / iStock: Rainer von Brandis (bl). NASA: NOAA (cra). 130 Alamy Stock Photo: Joerg Boethling (crb); Josie Elias (cb). Getty Images / iStock: Androsov (clb). 131 Alamy Stock Photo: Anthony Pierce (clb). Dreamstime.com: Larisa Blinova (tl); David Pereiras Villagra (cb). Getty Images / iStock: E+ / Moyo Studio (crb). 132 naturepl.com: Ralph Pace (crb). 133 Alamy Stock Photo: Barbara Ash (bl). 134 Dreamstime.com: Ig0rzh (bl). 134–135 123RF.com: Iakov Kalinin. Alamy Stock Photo: Robertharding / Michael Runkel (cb). 135 Alamy Stock Photo: Arterra Picture Library / De Meester Johan (tl); FLHC 3 (tr); BIOSPHOTO / Sylvain Cordier (cl); Jesse Rockwell (cb); WaterFrame_fba (b); Adisha Pramod (ca). 136 Alamy Stock Photo: MasPix (cl). Dreamstime.com: Linda Bair (crb); Tirrasa (cra). 136–137 123RF.com: Iakov Kalinin. Alamy Stock Photo: Nature Photographers Ltd / Paul R. Sterry (tl). Dreamstime.com: Fonciw (ca). 137 Dreamstime.com: Goldghost (tc). NASA: Goddard Modis Rapid Response Team (cra). 140 Dreamstime.com: Derek Rogers (b). 141 Dreamstime.com: Tirrasa (tl)

Cover images: Front: Alamy Stock Photo: RooM the Agency / seanscott; Dreamstime.com: Paul Banton / Paulbanton72 cl; Back: Alamy Stock Photo: imageBROKER / J.W.Alker cra.

All other images © Dorling Kindersley
For further information see: www.dkimages.com